CW01499005

SAINTS AND SCHOLARS

Gavin Gregan

authorHOUSE®

AuthorHouse™ UK Ltd.
500 Avebury Boulevard
Central Milton Keynes, MK9 2BE
www.authorhouse.co.uk
Phone: 08001974150

First published by AuthorHouse 2/17/2010

ISBN: 978-1-4490-7062-5 (sc)

"The best hope of a nation lies in the proper education of its youth"

— Erasmus, circa 1500 AD

Do It Now

"Until one is committed, there is hesitancy, the chance to draw back. Concerning all acts of initiative (and creation), there is one elementary truth, the ignorance of which kills countless ideas and splendid plans: that the moment one definitely commits oneself, then Providence moves too. All sorts of things occur to help one that would never otherwise have occurred. A whole stream of events issues from the decision, raising in one's favor all manner of unforeseen incidents and meetings and material assistance, which no man could have dreamed would have come his way. Whatever you can do, or dream you can do, begin it. Boldness has genius, power, and magic in it. Begin it now."

A Vision of the Future

It is my hope and my belief, that your generation, the next generation will become a generation of collaborative, creative, independent entrepreneurs who provide a valuable service in exchange for an agreed fee and who provide that service at the highest possible quality.

It is my hope and my vision, that each of you can bring your own unique values, vision, sense of self and philosophies to whatever it is that you do.

It is my hope that you will not be constrained by any of the mistakes of our past, but that you help to create a real paradigm shift in what it means to be Irish, and what it means to be an individual, as part of the whole.

At the very least, I hope that you will live your life being true to yourself and with a real sense of authenticity, and you will bring that authenticity, self-awareness and unique talents to bear in every area of your life, whether that be educational, professional, family, sporting or whatever else.

The world is now yours to inherit and if our best hope lies in the hands of your generation, then it is also possible that you best hope lies in our generation to some degree and I hope that this book is of some assistance.

Contents

Introduction

Take a look around you. Unless you have lived in a cave for the past couple of years, you would be under no illusion that this isn't exactly a glorious period in Irish or World history.

Put in plain language, things are a little shit at the moment aren't they?

You can hardly open a newspaper anymore because, quite frankly, it's not going to put you in a very positive frame of mind for the rest of your day is it?

But all is not lost.

Yes, mistakes have been made and mistakes will be made again I'm sure.

The mistakes which were made don't take away from the possibilities and the potential that still exists for us all, do they?

Here's the important fact. In 10-20 years, you and your generation will be the leaders of our country, and indeed our world.

You will be the bankers, parents, politicians and more of the future. Don't be scared. That's the reality.

You shall inherit this country and this world, with its beauty and its ugliness, its potential and its hangovers from previous mistakes.

Our hope lies in your hands, as strange as it may sound. We cannot improve and build our future by constantly looking over our shoulders to the mistakes of the past. That will give us a linear progression and greater chance of repeating old mistakes, because we will simply re-learn the old and wrong ways of doing things.

What we need is a quantum shift, a complete paradigm shift as individuals, as communities, as a country and beyond, because no matter your nationality, we are not really all that different, if we choose to be.

It is you who must shape our future and that will involve sometimes listening to "our" generation and sometimes, completely ignoring what we say and going with your own gut, your own mind, your own heart. And that's what this book is about.

This book is about helping you to build your own mind, heart and instincts, so that the future is built not on the mistakes of the past but on your dreams of the future.

It is my hope and my vision that the Ireland of the future and indeed the world of the future is in the hands of a new generation, you, who have the ambition, the passion to make things better for everyone.

It is my hope that Ireland enters a new era of Saints and Scholars, led by you, and supported by us, where appropriate, the generation before but that ultimately you become individuals and teams of people with greater self-awareness than we did, greater certainty than we did and to firstly put Ireland back on the map for all the right reasons, but to use that position then for the good of all.

It is my hope that we emerge from this dark chapter in our history with a completely new mindset and with a quantum shift away from the past.

The opportunity is yours, and the challenge is yours also and I will challenge you in this book.

I will challenge you to become better than what came before you, and to become better than you were yesterday. I will challenge you to ask honest questions of yourself and I will challenge you to stretch a little from where you are today to be more tomorrow. I will challenge you to believe more about what you are capable of than you did yesterday. I will challenge you to question what you have learned from the generation which came before.

But I will support you also, as much as I challenge you.

Some of you will not accept this challenge, and that is ok. Some of you will prefer that the control of your life is in somebody else's hands, and some of you will continue to believe that there is no point in you making the effort, that you don't matter, and that nothing you do matters. You can believe that if you wish. But you will be wrong, because every change begins with one person. Every change must begin with you.

I'll ask you now, what do you want your life, and your country to look like in 10, 15, 20 years time. The only person who has direct control over what you choose now, is you.

So, read this book, consider it, and know that whatever else happens in the world, you are responsible for you and it is you who will live by your decisions in your life-time and by taking the lessons in this book on board, you will be in a better place than if you chose not to, and it is my hope that we will all be in a better place because of it.

Who is this book for?

Quite simply this book is for the future leaders of our country and our world. Primarily, that means the youth of today, but it doesn't have to be limited by age.

If you feel that you can be more, that your country should be a little better than it is, if you expect and demand more of yourself, your country and those around you, then this book is for you.

What the World Needs Now

I was running a workshop recently for young entrepreneurs, aimed at putting our minds together to create new ideas, new businesses perhaps which would not only bring out the best qualities and talents of the participants, but would also seek to meet a need out in the real world.

Times of recession have traditionally been times of great changes and innovation as we seem to be brought back down to basics and forced to re-assess our next direction in life.

Indeed, Hewlett Packard was founded during the depression of the 1930's and Microsoft was founded during the recession of the 1970's.

Recessions force us to think more creatively and to seek out new solutions to old and new problems. Recessions and depressions help us to discover quantum leaps and paradigm shifts in how we think and in how we view what is possible.

Perhaps this is because our backs are against the wall and the obstacles and excuses that normally exist for creative thinking and thrown to one side.

So anyway, during this brainstorming workshop, we began to ask ourselves, what does the world need now, what does our country need now, and what do people need now?

The answer to these questions of what we need produced some of the expected answers such as Green Energy, Food Sciences, Vaccines, Technology and more.

However, a couple of the more lateral thinking students actually pursued a more profound path.

What we are lacking more than ever now is not a scientific discovery, a new invention or a new bio-fuel.

What we are lacking now, and what our greatest need is, are human qualities.

Leadership, Inspiration, Hope, Direction and much more.

These are now our greatest needs, as aside from cold hard cash, these are what are missing most for us, individually, as a nation, and indeed as a people. Right now, our future, especially here in Ireland, has never been more uncertain as it is now.

As we enter into the "Knowledge Economy", we absolutely must increase our human qualities because it is precisely the lack of human qualities such as Honesty, Leadership, Responsibility, Emotional Intelligence and Inspiration that has caused this latest and incredibly challenging economic crisis.

It is precisely as a result of the lack of awareness, responsibility and emotional intelligence that we slipped into the global and societal hypnosis that allowed us to tolerate a financial and social system that lead us down this dangerous path.

But there is always a silver lining.

This upheaval has presented us with an opportunity for reflection, and an opportunity to change direction and to choose what future we wish to have for ourselves, not only here in Ireland, but globally.

What the world needs now is a new generation of leaders.

Where are our Heroes gone? Who are our Heroes? Should we even have Heroes or does having a Hero mean you have abdicated your own responsibilities and handed your power over to somebody else?

At the very least, perhaps we need role models, but who can be our role models currently? Who is there out there, in the economic, political or media arena that you could possible place on any pedestal right now?

I am presenting you with a challenge right now to accept yourself as the only true hero and role model you will turn to until you have at least finished reading the contents of this book. You will have mentors of course, as there are many people out there from whom you can learn at least one lesson, but keep in mind that you must make the decisions for yourself.

Yes, our parents may have done great things and have at the very least raised you to where you are now. But for now, open your mind to the realisation that you are approaching the threshold of adulthood and as such, your parents' role in your life is changing now, from one of carer and guardian to one of fellow human being and friend.

"When I was a boy of fourteen, my father was so ignorant I could hardly stand to have the old man around. But when I got to be twenty-one, I was astonished at how much the old man had learned in seven years."

- Mark Twain

The challenge is now yours to shape your life.

The world, more than ever, needs leaders to usher in a new era in communities, business and in politics and you are that next generation.

Are you ready?

You will be.

The State of the Nation

First, a brief history lesson, albeit, an unofficial version…

The Land of Saints and Scholars

The Land of Saints and Scholars signified a time in Irish History, after the arrival of Christianity when there was a cultural and artistic renaissance, ushering in a time of creative expression, a relative peace in the country (save a few minor skirmishes between a few local Chieftains), and when Ireland was indeed a powerhouse and a centre of education and research for all of Europe. Ireland was renowned throughout the known world for the quality of its centres of learning, its scientific research and its art.

It was between the years of 450-800 AD, give or take a few decades, nestled between the arrival of St Patrick and the first weekend shoppers from Scandinavia, also known as marauding Vikings.

We had a monastic community who were brilliantly composing iconic artistic works such as the Book of Kells, Book of Ulster and fashioning such iconic pieces of art, such as the Ardagh Chalice, the Derrynaflan Chalice, the Tara Brooch and many other priceless artefacts.

It was a time when the Christian monks used their knowledge, skill and art, to preserve the early records and copies of the bible in written form.

It was a time when Kings and Chieftains became patrons of local monasteries as centres of excellence for education and art.

Ireland became the "school" of Europe and the great Kings, Queens and Merchants of the known world sent their sons and daughters to be educated in the great Monastic schools of Ireland, such as Clonmacnoise and Glendalough.

It was during these years, coinciding with the fall of the Roman Empire, which also coincided with the Dark Ages, that many Irish monks such as Columbanus travelled across Europe, setting up monasteries and schools and maintaining and documenting historical records so that they would not be lost to the mists of time.

It was a time when it is largely acknowledged that the Irish monks to a great extent, saved civilisation[1], as it was known, and maintained knowledge and culture for future generations.

This era of the Land of Saints and Scholars was truly a glorious period in Irish history.

As a means of an even more amateur and simplistic view on our history since then, consider the following.

---

1   Look for a book called "How the Irish Saved Civilisation", by Thomas Cahill

It all came to an abrupt end when the Vikings arrived and from that moment on, Ireland eventually descended into a life of serfdom, in-fighting and division.

What followed were generations of subservience to various bodies of authority and being happy enough to live off the scraps from the master's table and, more ominously, blaming the master, and each other, for everything that went wrong.

So, fast forward through a thousand years or so, the Vikings came and stayed, the Normans came and stayed, the English came and, well, came and went to and fro, and still do to a great extent, thanks to Ryanair. (It's a good thing)

And then, when the English eventually "left" in terms of direct government, we started to "take care of ourselves", or at least that's the theory.

And that brought us into the 20th and 21st century, where we established ourselves as a nation in the world eventually and experienced the "Celtic Tiger" and what came after it.

Ireland 2010

So, what is the state of the nation, currently?

What we have left today resembles a nation of adolescents in a sense, with vicious and divisive sibling rivalry between the various sectors of our society.

We waited every year for a budget here and a pay-rise there to see what else our masters threw us from the top table.

When the master feeds us well, we are happy.

When he doesn't we are angry and resentful.

When the master makes lashings of food and wine (and opiates) available, we enjoy copiously, gain great girths, adopt addictions and generally, lose the run of ourselves, and all the while, giving the master back the very pay he only just threw into our beggar's bowl.

And so finally, the master decides that the time of plenty comes to an end and he can no longer afford to throw us his scraps.

And we get bitter, resentful and so on and so forth.

So, what does this all mean to you?

Well, firstly, to be fair, we are a pretty young country in the greater scheme of things, so let's not be too hard on ourselves.

The Celtic Tiger was our first taste of what it would be like if we all had greater relative wealth and, to be fair, we hadn't a clue how to handle it. I'll give you a taster of a phrase which will be mentioned much more throughout this book.

We didn't have the Emotional Intelligence to handle the money the way it came.

What's done is done however and I'm not here to give an Economics lecture.

What I will point out however is that I'm not sure we ever really threw off our Imperial Hangover. At least not yet.

One quite comical thing that I noticed during our rise to riches during *The Tiger* was that our official wealth figures were continuously being compared with our UK neighbours.

What on earth for? Were we still so insecure in ourselves that we had to keep comparing ourselves to our "Ex" that lived over the road?

As if that wasn't enough, internally, we were forever comparing what we had with our immediate neighbours!

If he built a deck, then by God, so will I.

They bought an apartment where? Where's that? Do Ryanair fly there? Right so, we're having one too!

My point, can we please stop comparing ourselves to our neighbours and get our own garden sorted?

Can we now, make a decision to draw a line in our history about such ways of thinking?

This is one challenge you have.

Can you make a promise to yourself, that what you consider to be enough for you, good enough for you in your life, is based on a set of real values that you decide, and not about what your neighbour has or what somebody else has?

Choose now to define your own sense of value, and of enough, based on what you truly want in your life, and I promise you, that will have a great bearing on all aspects of your life.

Throughout the rest of your life, although you feel as if you may be competing with others, whether that be in school, sports, or later in business and career, you are not.

99% of the time, your life will be spent competing with your inner obstacles, comfort zones and demons.

Forget about the external competition at least until you are 100% clear on what is going on inside first.

The reason our country is in the mess it is in, is because we have spent our entire history[2] comparing ourselves and what we have, to our neighbour, be that the neighbour next door or across the water.

Make a promise now, to yourself, to get your own house in order and the rest will take care of itself.

---

2   This is not intended as a statement of historical fact, in case you feel the need to write to the Irish Times.

So Where to Next?

We have come to a point in our nation's history, and indeed, world history, where never before has there been more of a need and a demand of ourselves and from ourselves to **be** more as people.

With the changing economic, political and cultural climate, worldwide, this is the perfect and essential time to pause, reflect and take stock of how far we have come and where we wish to go next.

Never before, in recent history, has there been a time, when we need to stop and ask ourselves:

Who are we, where are we going, what do we stand for and what do we want?

And indeed looking forward:

Who do we want to be, where do we want to go, what do we want to stand for and what do we want to have in our lives?

As a people and as a nation, what are the values and what *is* the value of modern Ireland?

It all begins with us, as individuals. It begins with you, as an individual.

What do you want? What do you believe you should stand for and what do you believe your country should stand for? What is important to you?

The maxim is clear.

If we wish to have more, we must do more and if you wish to do more, we must be more.

What we *choose to be* dictates what we are capable of doing and capable of having; as individuals, as communities and as a country.

No man or woman is an island, so if you want to have more personally, we need to begin thinking bigger, and thinking outside ourselves to the wider community and the country as a whole.

After a decade of indulgence and excess in every manner imaginable, it is now vital to be clear and to be certain what each of us now really stands for and what we intend to create next.

If we no longer have our Porsches, our Spanish villas and our stock portfolios, we must find our certainty and sense of who we are somewhere else and in something else[3].

What are our real values?

Nay, what *is* our real Value?

In a world of Global Economics where the slide is downwards towards cheaper labour and goods, what is our Value, what is **your** Value?

Already, at least one Multinational has indicated that its sojourn in what was once a cheap labour market is over. More may follow. More will follow.

---

3   I love Porsches, but your sense of self cannot be dependent on it. It's for fun and enjoyment ☺

But is it useful, productive and mature of us to always expect a large corporation to come in and *give* us jobs, even accepting the benefits of Foreign Direct Investment?

For years, we had full employment, everyone had a job. What are your expectations now?

450,000 unemployed and 200,000 of those people joined the queue since 2008. It was quick and it was vicious.

Do we believe that 200,000 jobs will appear out of nowhere all of a sudden?

I don't believe so.

I believe that this gap of 200,000 will take time to close, but it will close. It won't be because of massive Foreign Direct Investment from multi-nationals. It will come from enterprising people here, at home.

It will come from thousands of small businesses who create 10 jobs here, 20 jobs there in the form of partnerships, in collaboration.

It will happen when there is less inward competing with each other and more collaboration, co-operation and trust between business ventures.

Yes, we do need large scale Irish success stories to rival the Googles and Facebooks of the world, but it needs to begin, as they did, with 1 or 2 enterprising geniuses, who had a dream and followed it and the rest is history.

Even Bill Gates and Steve Jobs began their journeys in their parents' garage.

As ironic as it sounds, we need to dream big but take baby steps.

As I will address further on, we need to change our thinking at every level and that includes our notion of "getting a job".

The day is gone when we are guaranteed a job for life. It is accepted as fact that people will have at least 14 jobs in their lifetime. This could also change. People are looking at having numbers of complete career changes in their lives.

We need to take a step back from the bad press the country is getting because it's not really conducive to creative thinking is it? We're constantly being told that we're the laughing stock of the EU and perhaps the world.

That's not much of a way to throw off an inferiority complex is it?

We need to re-define what we are capable of, what we wish to do with our lives and align ourselves with our capabilities and values in order to shape our lives.

We are capable of so much more than is currently apparent, but you need to believe you are and you need to decide you are.

The landscape is constantly changing, and the only constant in that cycle of change is you, in terms of who you believe you to be, and what you believe to be important to you, regardless of what chaos there is in the outside world.

In a sense, the global crisis is providing us with the opportunity to slow down, take stock, simply because everything seems to be stuck currently and going nowhere fast.

The only way truly is up from here and in a twisted way, if you are to believe that there is no guaranteed business or job out there waiting for you, then you may as well start making decisions based on what you love to do and what you are good at, instead of being herded into the cattle trucks marked "IT", "Financial Services", or whatever else just because they're the growth areas.

Everyone needs to be IT savvy, everyone needs to be financially savvy, but you all don't need to base your careers in it, in order to benefit from the opportunities in it.

Open your mind now to what you really love to do, what you are good at and use this time in your life to make a better choice for you and your life into your future.

Your Challenge

A Return to Eden

There's only one corner of the universe you can be certain of improving, and that's your own self.

- Aldous Huxley

It is time to usher in a new era of Saints and Scholars, and it is you, the next generation, who must be those Saints and the Scholars.

Again, this goes beyond Ireland, this is a global need.

We have had our decades of corruption, greed, banking crises and more, and although I accept that this is neither your fault and you may be very apathetic about it, the fact is that you are the next generation, and it is up to you to stand up and be counted, and to stand up and start making decisions first for yourself, and secondly for the wider community.

You can choose.

Do you want the Ireland and the world of the future to be shaped by the mistakes of the generations that came before or do you want it to be shaped by you, and built upon the many positives we have as a nation and a people?

A time where we hold *ourselves* up to the highest of principles, the highest of virtues, the highest of standards and the loftiest of values.

This is Saints and Scholars in the sense of hearts and minds and purpose.

By Saint, I mean being guided from within, from your heart, from your own highest values, principles and moral code.

By Scholars, I mean applying your keen intellect, the power and focus of your mind to plan your life, make decisions and take committed action and most importantly deciding to take responsibility for everything we do, individually and collectively.

If we are to build a Knowledge Economy, we must first develop the people that form that knowledge economy. A Knowledge Economy however also needs to be built on a foundation of clear values, guiding principles and vision.

Before you allow that voice in your head to tell you that you have nothing to offer, that you cannot possibly make a difference, know one thing.

The only people that *can* make a difference are individuals. First one, then two, and before you know it, when ten people share the same idea or ideals, a quorum is achieved and something begins to happen.

But you must take the first step in yourself.

There is no such thing as a human without potential. There is no such thing as a human without a talent or skill.

There is a very common thing called wasted potential and un-used skill however.

Everybody and I mean everybody has a talent, and the ability to use that talent.

Perhaps our mistake has been to always wait for the correct monetary award to express it.

Perhaps we've decided to hide our talents and skills until we get paid for it.

Perhaps we have hidden our talents in case we get laughed at by somebody.

What a mistake to make.

Evolution dictates that you must "use it or lose it". If you are hiding your talents, you are only cheating yourself, not to mention the wider community.

There are millions of stories about wasted talent, unfulfilled potential and dreams that simply faded away.

Make a choice now that this will not include you.

Choose now, to apply yourself, for yourself.

It has been said that persistence, determination and the application of effort is more valuable than talent, and psychologists are not at all convinced about the notion of "natural" talent anyway, although history has thrown up true child prodigies.

You can take confidence from the fact that focus of intention, a sense of purpose, determination and a never say die attitude can achieve far more than any notion of "talent".

Anybody can learn computer programming or financial services or any other technical skills. That's easy. Our minds are super computers and technical skills are easy to learn (from a good teacher).

A greater challenge is to build on your personal skills and other areas of intelligence. In a later chapter, I'll expand on this, but my point is that it is far more important for your life and for the future of the country and indeed the world, that our broader qualities and intelligence is developed in terms of Personal Awareness, Emotional Intelligence, Social Awareness and more.

Technical Skills and Financial genius count for nothing unless they are based on a foundation of maturity and wisdom.

At the outset, I told you that I will challenge you, but that I will also support you.

I challenge you now, to accept this mission if you like and later on, we can look at how to first of all overcome the inner obstacles that might be holding you back or keeping you in a less than productive place, and then we'll look at how you can, really, practically, begin to make a difference in your life, in your family and then beyond.

It only takes little steps, but consistently taking those little steps in the right direction will bring exponential results.

Saints and Scholars points to a new energy, a new momentum where our people, young or old, but especially the young, are a blend of high principles, clear values, keen focus and applied endeavour and efforts.

There can be no recession on a personal level when you choose to begin a journey from within yourself.

And once such a journey has begun, you will be very surprised at how many of the "problems" and worries of life melt away and no longer appear on your radar.

For those of you who may be prone to blaming external forces for how life has turned out so far, consider this:

When you change your focus to look for your inner guidance and focus on what YOU personally can do to control, create and shape your own life, you'll realise that all those hours you spent blaming friends, parents, politicians and other "powers" for controlling and spoiling your life were unnecessary and frankly a complete waste of your precious time.

We cannot rail against our politicians and bankers if we ourselves have no idea what we stand for and if we ourselves do not measure up to a standard that we set for ourselves.

It *is* ironic that our "representatives" do accurately represent us, and who can argue that the bickering, greed and loss of direction and values which we have witnessed is not exactly a true representation of what we have largely become.

We are only angry at our leaders because we ourselves abdicated our responsibility for our own lives and destinies and trusted others to do it for us and to throw us the scraps.

We were the ones who fell asleep at our own wheels and left it to others to take care of us.

Why waste time being angry unless you do something to change it?

We become what we tolerate. Indeed, we became what we tolerated.

They were merely the busy parents trying to balance the books and pay the mortgage, while we were the presumptuous teenagers (metaphorically) who always assumed there would be a roof over our heads, and a hot dinner when we came home.

But like in all real families, there comes a day when you have to roll your sleeves up and plough your own furrow.

You are at the point in your lives now, where you are shaping your view of the world, defining your values and your place in the world even if that is happening unconsciously.

Are you going to continue to be one of the herd, or are you going to begin your own journey to who you really are?

If this is to be a new revolution, then unlike the French Revolution, the only heads that need to roll are our own.

We need to get our own heads straight to get our lives straight.

Thomas Jefferson actually believed that there should be a revolution every two to three generations to ensure that there is no risk of tyranny or of one influence becoming too powerful in society.

This also serves to keep things fresh and to keep any part of society from becoming complacent.

Every civilization has been through it.

Thankfully, there are milder revolutions that can happen, and not only physical and bloody ones.

There needs to be a revolution on a personal level for us all, emotional and mental.

The only revolution we need right now in within ourselves, to take real responsibility for our own philosophies, our own principles, our own beliefs, and most of all, our own thoughts and actions.

No more waiting for "them up there" to fix things for us.

Ireland is a comparatively young nation, though an ancient land. The last decade or so, I believe has been our adolescence, an aberration of sorts, where we enjoyed excess and never gave a thought for tomorrow.

The entire country went through life in the same way as a boy-racer drives. We had no consideration about what might be coming around the next corner and we had the arrogance to believe that it would also be in our favour, regardless of our own choices and actions.

We are now at the beginning of a new cycle in our evolution and maturation, where we must now begin to make improved conscious choices.

I do believe that a change for the better is on the way and I do hope and believe that we have learned some lessons and will come through these times more self aware and with more personal responsibility.

Right now, we need to stand up and wake up.

Your families and communities need you to stand up and wake up.

Your country needs you to stand up and wake up.

What are the new standards we will set for ourselves as individuals and as a country?

What can we become and what shall we become as individuals and as a country?

What do you want?

Your Opportunity

Your opportunity is clear

The earth is yours to inherit, literally. There is almost a wasteland around you at present and much like in the legends of King Arthur, people are waiting for someone to emerge from the wilderness.

The Arthurian legends talked of virtue, honour and the notion of service to a higher cause as being the manner in which the darkness would disappear and the new era would arrive.

The Holy Grail in fact has been described by some scholars as simply signifying a Code of Honour. The Grail Code, being of service, following clear values and a sense of honour.

It was their belief that original Kings and Queens ruled by the Grail Code and saw themselves truly as servants of the people.

However, power corrupts as we all know and this code of honour disappeared over time.

There are members of governments who do have aspirations of service and contribution, something akin to the Grail Code, but there are not enough.

Your opportunity is to define your own Grail Code, understand it, follow it and truly inherit the earth.

Again, the simple facts are that you shall be the next generation whether you like it or not. How do you want to lead? Decide now. What world do you want for yourselves and future generations?

It begins with you.

How well do you know yourself? Where is your sense of honour? Where is your sense of Service? What higher cause outside of yourself do you value? What aspects within yourself do you value?

Decide now to be the best you can be.

Decide now what values you shall honour.

Decide now what you stand for and what shall make you unique and even at your young age, decide now, what will you be remembered for?

Our greatest Asset

We are a small land mass, with no significant natural resource in terms of Gas, Oil or precious metals.

The amount we do have is not sufficient to make us self-sufficient, not to mention having enough for export, and the fact that commodities are internationally traded, we can't even keep our own gas and give it away for free!

Our greatest asset always has and probably always will be our people and the skills and resources they possess.

And, it goes a step further.

Not only is it the skill-set and the natural resources of our people that is essential but it is the human quality of our people also and the sense of wisdom (and at least until recently) and sense of genuine humility which often set the Irish apart as being wonderful ambassadors wherever we travelled.

The fact that we have never been involved in a major armed conflict with another nation, or invaded another nation (not since Niall of the Nine Hostages abducted St Patrick that is) also places us well as Ambassadors and Statesmen and women.

These qualities should not be under-estimated as they are what place us at a real and distinct advantage in the new global economy.

We no longer have a cheap labour market when compared with emerging nations.

We no longer will have a major manufacturing industry.

It is our people that are our greatest asset and we need to develop this even more.

We need to develop ourselves even more, on every level.

There is no point in developing infrastructure or property if we do not also, or indeed, first, develop our people.

To have a developed infrastructure without a developed people would be like building a 6 star hotel for monkeys, though I run the risk of being unkind to monkeys.

We need to adopt the frame of mind where we seek to develop world class people, and that begins with you, on an individual level, deciding to be a world class individual, with a world class philosophy, making truly excellent choices and always being on top of your game, whatever that game may be.

A return to humility is essential. There is no disgrace in being underestimated and humble but also wise.

To be humble does not mean to be subservient. To be humble is the greatest expression of confidence.

Humility is essential especially when things are going well.

As an old Irish saying goes, "*you must walk carefully when carrying a full jug!*"

I believe that we lost our humility during the economic boom.

I believe the fact that we lost our humility damaged us as a people somewhat.

Our loss of humility gave rise to the corruption and greed which we have witnessed in the banking sector, scandals which have damaged our international reputation, and which in my mind are an Offence against the State.

Increased mental, emotional and even spiritual intelligence and maturity is our requirement as a nation. This needs to be embraced, harnessed and utilised in a manner that enables us to think globally but to grow and act locally.

These philosophies can be extended further to say that an Ireland built on these principles and ideals is a necessity for the world and a stronger, wiser Ireland is not only good for Ireland but good for the world.

It's time to look at Ireland and her people in a new light and look beyond the wind down of manufacturing, see ourselves as more than new consumers and begin to embrace a new and bolder image and expectation of ourselves.

This may not be easy for the older generations but it can be done, and in particular it falls to our younger generation to be the new, bold ambassadors of our country, but first, you need to become the ambassador of yourself.

First, you build from the bottom up, from the inside out and that's where true certainty and confidence comes from.

And that is the direction this book is going to take next. I've explained to you why we need you.

I've also explained to you the opportunity that awaits you.

Now, we're going to Bootcamp to get you into the right shape to take on the challenge.

Rudyard Kipling
If

If you can keep your head when all about you
Are losing theirs and blaming it on you;
If you can trust yourself when all men doubt you,
But make allowance for their doubting too;
If you can wait and not be tired by waiting,
Or, being lied about, don't deal in lies,
Or, being hated, don't give way to hating,
And yet don't look too good, nor talk too wise;

If you can dream - and not make dreams your master;
If you can think - and not make thoughts your aim;
If you can meet with triumph and disaster
And treat those two imposters just the same;
If you can bear to hear the truth you've spoken
Twisted by knaves to make a trap for fools,
Or watch the things you gave your life to broken,
And stoop and build 'em up with wornout tools;

If you can make one heap of all your winnings
And risk it on one turn of pitch-and-toss,
And lose, and start again at your beginnings
And never breath a word about your loss;
If you can force your heart and nerve and sinew
To serve your turn long after they are gone,
And so hold on when there is nothing in you
Except the Will which says to them: "Hold on";

If you can talk with crowds and keep your virtue,
Or walk with kings - nor lose the common touch;
If neither foes nor loving friends can hurt you;
If all men count with you, but none too much;
If you can fill the unforgiving minute
With sixty seconds' worth of distance run -
Yours is the Earth and everything that's in it,
And - which is more - you'll be a Man my son!

Your Bootcamp

We've covered the history lesson, the political lecture, a bit of socio-economics and you're still here. Take a bow. I'm sure there were times when you almost gave up.

But not so, and your rewards shall be great…

The next part of this book enters the world of Life Coaching to some degree but with a dose of reality.

If our hope and intention is that the next generation will take up the challenge of creating a better society, better businesses and a better everything, then the first steps, the changes have to come from you the individual.

Because of this basic fact, the next section is devoted to you, as an individual, to try to help you become a better more effective young person who can then take those strengths and work with others.

The next section is in fact a mini Self Help book.

If you were a private client, sitting in front of me, we would have the benefit of dialogue, questions, answers and more probing questions to get to the heart of you, and to get to the heart of what you want.

Unfortunately, we are not sitting face to face, so for that reason, I am going to challenge you a bit more. At times, it may seem like I'm slapping your wrists and pushing your buttons, but it's all a means to awaken the real you, and to get you to be honest with yourself and move to a new level.

Only after you have enjoyed this section, and you will enjoy it, can you sit down and really start to plan things for yourself, and set goals and begin to build your life.

So forget about changing the world just for now, and forget about fixing all of the country's problems.

For now, let's deal with you as an individual.

Buckle up, and enjoy the ride.

A journey of a thousand miles begins with a single step.

- Lao-tzu

The Next Generation

I'd like to address the audience if you don't mind…

Hands up who agrees with the following statement:

Now, as you all well know, none of you are mature enough, wise enough or intelligent enough to plan your own life or make your own decisions for how your life is going to develop over the next 10 years.

For this reason, all responsibility for your decision-making rests in the hands of your friends, your parents, your teachers, the government and all future employers.

Now the good thing about this is that whenever anything goes wrong in your life, you'll be able to blame any of the above, because it is never going to be your fault. All you need to do is continue to say yes to everyone and follow the herd.

Your reaction to this paragraph will shape the rest of your life more than you can ever imagine…

So, be honest with yourself, did you find yourself wanting to agree with that in anyway?

Did you find yourself thinking "Eh, no, I make my own choices!"

Now is the time for you to sit up and start paying attention and realise that in 10 years time when you find yourself stuck in some rut, disappointed that life didn't turn out how you had planned, there's no point in blaming the rest of the world.

You can feel angry and frustrated, that's allowed, but there's no point in directing that anger and frustration at the world. Do something about it. Focus that frustration and get back on the horse.

You have more than enough time, resources and imagination to choose the life you want now and whether you have realised it or not, you are the one who must live and die by your thoughts, words and actions.

This point can't be stressed enough.

You are no longer a child. Your parents and teachers had the job to guide you to this point and now you have to make the correct choices that produce a life that you really can be proud of and happy with.

You are the artist and the architect of your life and every thought, word and action is a brick in the wall of what will be your life.

The rest of the world may try to influence and affect you, but ultimately it's your reaction to your world that dictates the life you live.

Ultimately your goal is to make your life a creation, an expression and a reflection of all that is good about you.

Is your life currently living up to your expectations and do you feel that your life is a reflection of who *you* are or are you still following the herd?

Is your life following a direction of your choosing or do you feel like a small boat tossed about by the wind and high seas?

Don't worry if you start to panic because you haven't yet even begun to wonder who you are.

This is the beginning of the journey, and all you need right now, is a curiosity and a willingness to play the lead role in the drama, the epic, the comedy that can be your life.

And why wouldn't you? You are the lead role aren't you? If not you, then who?

If you are already rolling your eyes to heaven, thinking "whatever", remember, it's your imagination that is the key here.

You need to take a step back and realise that in front of you is a blank canvass, no matter what has happened so far and no matter how your life is now.

Tomorrow has not happened, so you have a choice, but you need to make a choice, not just coast along on a whim.

You can repeat yesterday's mistakes and make tomorrow just another Groundhog Day or you can take stock of what has brought you this far and ask yourself "is this what I want for myself, for my life? If I could choose, what would I do next? How do I want tomorrow to be? How do I wish today to be?"

As a child, you had no limits on your imagination, you never settled for less than the most magnificent dreams and you had total certainty that they would come true. Not belief, but actually certainty.

Well, it may sound ironic, but for you to take the best step forward into your future, and to create a future full of expansion, growth and possibility, instead of a future of predictable limitation and frustration, you need to have the mind of a child, with an open-ended and unlimited ability to imagine and to kick all cynicism and scepticism into touch because all they do is limit you.

Let your mind play as you begin to imagine what future really does serve you and what future really represents who you are.

The fact is the external world will throw up enough limitations anyway, so make sure that you don't start placing limitations in your own mind.

As Al Pacino said in *Two for the Money*, "**keep pushing until something pushes back, and then push a little more**."

The world with its 6.7 billion inhabitants (and counting) is going to resist you anyway, so don't help them in being your own enemy or your own critic either.

Become your own best friend. Anything else is a little insane. But don't forget, best friends don't let friends do really stupid things!

The one place where you have absolute dominion and control, the place where you are King and Queen, and Emperor and Empress is in your own mind, so no limits, enjoy it, have fun with it and it will give you back the same fun ten-fold.

You and only you can decide what to think about and what to place your attention on.

Yes, it is true that not all of your dreams will manifest, but that doesn't matter.

Simply by keeping your mind full of thoughts that are of a positive nature has benefits for your health and keeps you young at heart.

In the same way that the majority of the benefits that stemmed from the NASA space program had nothing to do with space travel, but instead included advancements made in medicine, the invention of disposable hypodermic needles (which helped eliminate many diseases from the world), the same can apply to pursuing your dreams.

Sure, you just may not get to the original finishing post in every race you run, but you can be guaranteed that along the way you will get a hundred other benefits.

It's your mind, use it as you please and use it in a way that suits you and works for you.

If it sounds a little bit delusional, then great. A sprinkle of well focused alleged delusion has played a part in most of the greatest seismic shifts in human history. It all began with a genius/madman (or woman) thinking in an independent fashion and daring to be different.

By opening up your mind again to the playful day-dreaming that everyone is capable of, you can then begin to put a form on those thoughts and dreams and to shape them into action that will eventually shape your life.

There are some principles you really need to become aware of here and now.

- Your life is shaped by actions

- Your actions are shaped by your thoughts and beliefs

- Your thoughts and beliefs are shaped by your values and philosophies in life.

In all of this, and in creating your "every day", your imagination plays an important part.

Think about it. The day ahead hasn't happened, so for you to think about it, and things that haven't yet happened, you need to imagine them.

How you imagine your day and life ahead is shaped by your philosophies, your beliefs and some past events.

How the day ahead pans out is for the most part shaped by how you imagined it and how you expected it to be and so you get into a vicious cycle.

The task, for you, is to stop acting on auto-pilot and begin to imagine and decide how you do want today and tomorrow to be.

To achieve this, we'll look at your current philosophy about yourself and life, and maybe a change is needed there.

We'll look at your beliefs and attitudes about you and about life, and maybe a change or an adjustment is needed there.

And then you'll find that some of your decisions will be different, as will some of your actions as you discover new beliefs about you and your life.

No Imagination?

"Imagination is more important than knowledge. For while knowledge defines all we currently know and understand, imagination points to all we might yet discover and create."

- Albert Einstein

Many people claim that they have no imagination, yet everyday they get out of bed and they "imagine" how the day ahead is going to be, and they "expect" bad things to happen, and they "just know" how things always turn out.

No imagination eh? Everyone has an imagination and unfortunately most people are using the incredible power of their imagination to imagine exactly what they DON'T want, which again, unfortunately only guarantees that what they DON'T want will materialise.

People who say they have no imagination still fall out of bed in the morning "assuming" that today will be just like yesterday. That's using your imagination in ALL the wrong ways.

If you spend your time focusing on your problems and limitations, then your life is dominated by those problems and limitations.

Most things that occur in your life only occur in your mind, so do yourself a favour and start focusing on some good stuff and if you dig deep enough, there's always something good there.

These same imaginative thoughts are what are already guiding every moment of your life, so pay attention to them and begin cultivating thoughts that are helpful to you and your life.

Again, most people's experience of life is not what actually happens "out there" but how it is represented in your mind. So if you've been replaying the same old CDs over and over again, change the tune and re-load a new soundtrack.

A golden rule of life and of existence is (and I'll repeat this over and over again until you're repeating it yourself):

If you want to have more, you must do more and if you want to do more, you must be more.

So, the questions are posed to you here, now and the answers to these questions will shape the direction of your life. And even if you don't choose conscious answers, then the existing unconscious patterns that exist for you will dominate.

Who do you want to be in your life?

What do you want to do in your life?

What do you wish to have in your life?

So, starting today, using your imagination and your vision for yourself, what do you wish to Be?

When you choose to be something grand enough, you can then easily imagine and choose doing greater things, and then having better things will come naturally.

All behaviour and learning is state dependant i.e. your state of mind.

You can hardly imagine "doing" the work of a CEO, or Surgeon or President if you imagine yourself "being" bored, useless, talentless, unhappy etc?

But it needs to start with being something better, being something new.

The greater the dream of Being, the more you aim to Be, the greater choice you have to Do more and doing and having more will be far easier and productive.

So, choose now, what do you wish to Be today? **Who** do you wish to Be today?

Once upon a time there was a wise man who used to go to the ocean to do his writing. He had a habit of walking on the beach before he began his work. One day he was walking along the shore. As he looked down the beach, he saw a human figure moving like a dancer. He smiled to himself to think of someone who would dance to the day. So he began to walk faster to catch up. As he got closer, he saw that it was a young man and the young man wasn't dancing, but instead he was reaching down to the shore, picking up something and very gently throwing it into the ocean. As he got closer he called out, "Good morning! What are you doing?" The young man paused, looked up and replied, "Throwing starfish in the ocean." "I guess I should have asked, why are you throwing starfish in the ocean?" "The sun is up and the tide is going out. And if I don't throw them in they'll die." "But, young man, don't you realize that there are miles and miles of beach and starfish all along it. You can't possibly make a difference!" The young man listened politely. Then bent down, picked another starfish and threw it into the sea, past the breaking waves and said, "It made a difference for that one."

You Can Only Control You

So, in starting a journey to change the world, and change society, where do you start?

Well, you can only start with you, and your main project will be in changing you.

As Ghandi put it:

"You must become the change you want to see in the world"

If we want the world to be more tolerant, honest and generous, then what we **don't do** is go out and order people to be more tolerant, honest and generous.

We start with ourselves.

The other obvious point is that the only person you can control and directly influence is yourself, and it is in changing yourself that you change your environment.

Trying to directly control or change other people is frustrating, next to impossible and nearly always doomed to failure.

As I have mentioned and will mention ad-nauseum, there are over 6 billion people in the world. It's an organised chaos that is rarely well organised.

The fastest and most guaranteed ticket to stress and anxiety is to either try to control other people, or to expect other people to behave in any particular way. Insanity in a bottle.

That's a battle you don't want to fight, trust me.

The first step to freedom and improvement in any form is to release everyone and everything else first.

The work begins with you.

The only person in this great big (shrinking) world that you can control or have responsibility for is you.

And believe you me, you will have a hard enough time controlling and managing *you* without worrying about other people.

When you do develop a good habit of effectively managing yourself then you will, indirectly, see many great ripple effects in your environment, and you will see yourself having a greater and more powerful influence on your environment.

The first step is *you* though. Work on *you*. Make *you* better. Hold your standards and values up high for *YOU* to aspire to and you'll be making a great stride forward.

When you have cultivated that sense of presence and certainty within yourself, other people will just sense it without you even saying anything. Your posture, your behaviour, the glint in your eye will tell a far greater story than words could tell.

Again, it's all about you becoming that Saint and Scholar.

When you begin to see you and your life as a real project, a lifelong project, where you strive to make today better than yesterday, and tomorrow better than today, life can only become better and take on a completely new meaning for you.

Later on, we'll get to the concept of your rules, your values, your philosophies and your principles, and how defining these and living by them, truly defines who you are and how your life is lived on those terms, your terms.

For now, it's sufficient for you to know that your life and your kingdom is *you*, and when you focus your beliefs, thoughts and actions on making you, making that kingdom as perfect and as powerful as you wish, change will have already begun, inside you and around you and for you.

You make the rules

"The greatest gifts you can give your children are the roots of responsibility and the wings of independence."

Denis Waitley

Like you, I hate being told what to do.

Like you, I hate people placing restrictions on my life.

I'm not a great fan of living my life according to somebody else's rules and plans either.

Having said all that, I do make things a little easier on myself in my "maturer years".

I know exactly what I **do** like to do.

I have a reasonable idea about what I consider to be right and wrong **for me**.

I try to remain conscious of my purpose each and every day, and I recognise that when I stray off track, something feels wrong inside me, so I take a step back.

I know my boundaries for my own behaviour (well, most times, I am human!) and I set clear boundaries for other people's behaviour towards me and my behaviour towards others.

I am reasonably aware (at this moment) of my own values, principles and passions in life. They can of course change.

I know what brings me joy and what brings me pain and I know which direction I prefer to lean between these two.

I can recognise when I'm *choosing* to be in a bad mood to gain some secondary benefit and I can recognise when I'm playing mind games with myself.

I choose to be honest with myself and to learn more about myself every day.

It wasn't always that way. There was a time when I was an angry young man, experiencing loads of "*bad luck*" and misfortune (at least that's how I saw it).

There was a time when it seemed like everyone around me was telling me what to do and how to behave.

There was a time when I'd listen to people telling me to be quiet and sit down.

There was a time when I received good advice and ignored it because it was just more noise and I was a stubborn young fool.

And then I woke up and started making my own clear rules for my life and all of a sudden the noise stopped and the "rulers" seemed to disappear. I sat down and I asked myself what I really cared about in life, what was really important to me, and made a decision to place those things at the centre of my own philosophy and hence my daily decisions.

I also allowed myself a degree of human error as life is not perfect.

And that's the key about this journey.

This book is not telling you what to do or how to do it.

You get to make your own rules.

You get to set the boundaries for your life, for your mind, your emotions, your interactions with others and your health and body.

You get to be in charge.

Nobody likes being told what to do, why would they? It's your life.

How on earth can anybody else be responsible for your thoughts, words and actions?

The people who may like to be in charge of you won't be paying your mortgage in years to come.

You will be the one to live and die, stand and fall by your decisions and actions.

And if you follow the steps in this book, you *will* be creating **your** rules for **your** life and eventually all the people who used to tell you what to do, all the people whose opinions you lived by, and all of the restrictions, limitations and frustrations will begin to disappear, or at least the controlling influence will.

What are you fighting for?

"My life has no purpose, no direction, no aim, no meaning, and yet I'm happy. I can't figure it out. What am I doing right?"

- Charles Schulz

Simply resisting all rules and rebelling **AGAINST** all authority is not big, clever or effective.

If you do want to fight, or feel the instinct to rebel, then fight **FOR** something, not **AGAINST** everything, because if you fight against something, you end up becoming that which you fight against.

Oddly enough, that was one of the downfalls of the French Revolution. The revolt was against everything, blind fury, so much so that great atrocities were committed and as there was no unifying vision to replace the old monarchical tyranny, chaos and anarchy ensued for some time.

Yes, it is absolutely part of being a teenager to rebel and resist authority because you are at the stage where you are asserting yourself and developing your ego.

But you now also have an opportunity to tweak evolution and bring in the power of intention and make conscious choices for yourself.

If you want real freedom, real independence and real opportunity to live your life your way, you need to decide on a real set of rules that you *do* agree with and not simply rebel blindly against those you don't like.

It's like creating your own constitution that works for you, but make sure it works for you, because if it doesn't really work in your best interests, it **WILL** have a knock on effect on those around you and then guess what...

Yes, "they", the rule makers, will have to intervene to control you again.

So, you get my point.

- No blind rebellions against everything

- Define your own set of rules that work in your real best interests.

- Discover what is really important to you and, yes, fight FOR it when necessary.

When you do this, as I said above, the rule makers will fade away and move on to the next rebellious enclave that is causing trouble.

Without wishing to bring politics into it, it's a bit like Israel and Palestine. Every now and then Israel allows Palestine to self-govern and promise to not re-invade Gaza as long as things remain stable.

Unfortunately, before too long, the peace breaks down, riots begin in Gaza, the Palestinian police find it difficult to maintain the peace and before you know it, the violence ends up on the streets of Tel Aviv, so one country's instability is now interfering with another.

And that's the point where the neighbour has to invade and place restrictions on movement, travel and freedom.

As a cautionary note, I do not know enough about the Middle East to have an informed opinion but this is merely an illustration of my point.

As an extra point, when I use the word "fight", it doesn't just mean taking to the streets. Most of the obstacles you face in life are actually internal, so when I say fight for what you believe in, that can simply mean, focus, work, apply yourself, put the effort in and move towards what it is that you want.

Your biggest opponent in life will always be inside of you, and learning how to say no, both to yourself and others, is also an important step.

If your behaviour is having a negative effect on other people, *they are going to try and restrict you. Why wouldn't they?*

However, once you begin to make real choices for yourself, which are really in your best interests, you will see huge positive change and clarity.

Sure, in the beginning, people around you won't be too keen on the fact that you are changing and improving, but that's only because they're afraid of being left behind and also because everyone and everything resists change initially.

As and aside, it is the way of the universe and nature to resist major change in order to preserve order.

This is what is known as homeostasis or the instinct to maintain the status quo and is a survival instinct.

Nature abhors both a vacuum and extremes, so it hates you doing nothing and also resists if you take on too much, so baby steps with certainty are the key.

1,000 small actions are more effective than an attempt at one huge step.

And don't worry, your friends and family will catch up eventually, if they so choose and if you stay focused on your passions in life and live and behave according to your guiding philosophy, values and principles, you'll get to where you're meant to be, regardless and you'll experience all of the benefits you are meant to experience.

Additionally, as you grow into becoming the real you, you'll cross paths with many other individuals on the same journey and that's where great ideas become world beaters. That's where you collaborate with like minds, and it's in that environment that the seeds of genius grow and spread and ideas become reality.

We are all individuals and we are all independent, but we are also interdependent with the entire planet in many ways.

It is also a great possibility that as you gain a better awareness of who you really are and what you value and cherish in life, that as you grow your social circle to include like-minded people that you may also find that other friends and acquaintances gradually drift away over time, and that's ok too.

Life moves on and life changes. Some changes you choose consciously, and some changes you do not, but you still "choose" to go with the flow. Again, life in many ways is purely a game of choices, each one taking you down a new road to a new crossroads.

The friends who are good for you, and who are meant to be in your life will remain and grow with you, and those who are not, well they'll go on their own journey.

As a quick exercise, imagine yourself in 30 years time in two forms.

One, where you held yourself back because you felt other people didn't want you to grow, change and achieve. Imagine that life, and imagine your level of fulfilment.

Alternatively, imagine yourself if you were in control of your own choices and destiny. Saying yes to you, yes to life.

Physically, you could still have the choice of the other life, but also all of the other experiences and gifts of life.

Never be afraid to make a choice. If it goes wrong, well then, make another one. If it goes right, guess what? Yes, make another one.

Too often we think that by choosing ONE thing, we automatically lose everything else. Not entirely true. Yes we lose some things, if we choose to, but the power of choice always gives you free will.

It is also true that to be decisive and to commit to something can mean cutting something out or saying no to something, but again, you have the choice and if you make your choices from a place of hope, optimism, passion and enthusiasm, as opposed to fear, doubt, pressure and panic, then your choices will always, on balance be right for you.

And remember, saying no to other people is in fact only a means of saying yes to you and there is no need for anyone to be offended. People may always do their best to make you feel guilty, but that's ok too. They were looking for something, they didn't get it and now, they have to find a new way to get it, because you exercised your right to choose and to say No.

The Dalai Lama once said that for offence to be caused takes two people.

One, to cause the offence, and the other to choose to be offended, so don't let misplaced guilt prevent you from making the right decision for your life because if something is not in your highest interests, it most certainly is not in other people's interests either.

Being a real hero

When I was growing up in the 80's, some of the films that I watched which had corny elements of heroism were movies like The Karate Kid, Rambo and generally the clichéd movies where a brave hero overcomes adversity etc etc to perform some outstanding heroic feat, more often than not to rescue a fair maiden or generally save somebody else's life..

As corny as the 80's were, don't knock these cinematic classics…

A lot of young men in particular, as they grow up, daydream about being a hero, whether on the football field, or on an imaginary battlefield.

In fact most of our myths and legends from the ancient Celts, through the Greek Classics involve great voyages of heroes seeking a great prize, a beautiful princess or a great castle.

The aforementioned Scholars have theorised that these great journeys were merely fables and metaphors for our journey through life (though taken from the male perspective because, sadly, history is told from the Paternal viewpoint, which is badly balanced).

As and aside consider this:

Young Hero – Young Man

Fair Maiden – Future Wife

Big Castle – Your House

Glittering Prize – Money

So, basically, these ancient legends were about the various stages of life and the pursuit of happiness.

You don't therefore need to be Jason and the Argonauts, Rocky Balboa, or King Arthur in order to lead a life of bravery and honour. As a point, there are sadly few documented examples of female "heroines" in ancient legends which is our loss.

The irony is that everyday, we are presented with innumerable opportunities to show real courage and to be a real hero, and to do the right thing for ourselves, by dealing with the simple things in life.

One of the best bits of advice I ever received was to not be so concerned with setting goal after goal after goal but instead to deal effectively with everything that comes your way.

Take part in life, participate and show up and you will have plenty of situations where valour, honour and courage are required.

Not in situations where your life is in danger or where you have to save some beautiful damsel in distress, but everyday situations where we have opportunities to stand up and say no to people or opportunities to make brave decisions that may not be glamorous but direct your life in tiny steps and in a way that can send your life in the correct direction that is for your benefit or perhaps not.

The toughest and bravest decisions you can currently make perhaps are those times when you have a choice to follow the herd, or follow your own direction. Standing out from the crowd is never easy, particularly as a teenager.

I think the main reason is that in order to have the self-confidence and the certainty to say no to a crowd, you need amazing self-awareness and self-knowledge.

The good news is that you're getting this here, now.

There are many world leaders who do not have such self-knowledge, self-awareness or emotional intelligence and are literally adrift in a sea of bad advice and poor decisions.

There will be an entire section later on real self confidence and self awareness, which you will find very useful.

With regards to being brave and making those everyday decisions, and dealing with what comes your way every day, it's the small steps with no obvious reward that have the most effect on our life direction and our character, and it is these habitual behaviours, which pass almost unnoticed, every day that have far more influence on our lives than any dramatic and heroic campaign.

Don't get me wrong by the way, life is still infinitely richer when you have grand dreams and visions which you aim to pursue, but when you set those visions and goals, it is still the baby steps that get you there.

Using the word No with ourselves and others is often the bravest challenge we shirk daily.

Checking our own habitual behaviours and choosing to stop an old outdated behaviour and try something new is often against our basic survival instincts.

We'll come back to the notion of saying No, and modifying your habitual behaviours later, but for now, keep in mind, that to be a hero and being brave involved a thousand little things and rarely 1 big thing.

As a little exercise, how many little activities do you repeat, every day, unconsciously without even thinking about them?

Little things like brushing your teeth, watching TV, snacking, smoking a cigarette, saying yes to everything your friends or family say.

Many of these habitual activities are of course vitally useful, such as brushing your teeth and in particular getting dressed before walking out the door, but many are not.

Many of those little habits have long become redundant and although served a purpose at one stage in your life, really have no benefit now.

Make out a list today and for each habit or activity, really ask yourself, ***do I need this anymore, is it serving any purpose?***

We'll come back to this in more detail later, but it's a good idea to drop it in now and have it ferment in the back of your mind.

What we have done so far is to provide you with a little wake up call, to let you know that you are responsible for you, and it is your choices that shape your life, and this starts here, now.

Let's continue and help you to get to know you a little better and there is much to learn.

The Power of Choice

"We are defined not by our personalities, but by our choices… We are condemned to freedom…"

– Jean-Paul Sartre

Jean-Paul Sartre was a famous existential philosopher. What he essentially meant by the lines above is that the most important and effective way to shape yourself, your life and your destiny is by making choices, by making decisions.

Choosing and deciding are not passive. They are actions, and there is a finality about a conscious decision and choice that takes your life in a new direction every time you make a committed decision.

He also noted that in doing so, that is, in choosing one thing, you have also "not chosen" the many other options and that is the price we pay for freedom, but it is also the greatest gift you have. Choice and free will, and with that, self-responsibility and accepting the results and consequences of your choices. We have much to learn on this point, individually and collectively.

Be assured, that although many people will try to influence your decisions, it is your life that will lead down a new highway when you make a choice, so when you make a choice, make it from your wisdom, from your heart.

By all means, listen to advice, listen to options, but then decide, based on what you believe to be right for you.

To the teenagers of Ireland, in 20 years time, you will be the doctors, politicians, law-makers, parents and leaders of this country, if you choose...

If you do not choose, you will continue to live your life blaming everyone else around you for how your life ended up.

If you do not choose, you will continue fighting with yourself and everyone around you, fighting until you have nothing.

If you do not choose, your life will shrink and reduce until it becomes a monotonous existence of limping along day to day.

The power of choice is wonderful isn't it?

If you do choose, then one of the wonderful things about your mind is that, every choice you make for yourself automatically and naturally builds your self-esteem without you even having to make that happen.

Every time you make a choice (by definitively saying yes or no to something) you give your life a direction and you shape your self and your life and each and every conscious decision and choice you make for the right reasons, builds your confidence and self esteem.

And no matter how difficult your current circumstances, if you cultivate the ingredients and develop an awareness of who you really are and what is really important to you, you will find a way.

Maybe right now, you're experimenting with different behaviours and pushing whatever sort of boundaries (and buttons) you can in some form of desperate rebellion. That's your choice right now.

True, every generation rebelled against something in some experimental way and in whatever way was considered extreme for that generation.

When your parents were young, they considered many things as taboo and extreme, which we consider "so like, normal, like"

Every generation, has an obligation to question the status quo, break the rules, and then rebuild things as they see fit.

That's evolution, and whether "we" like it or not, you will be running the country in 20 years, not your parents, so we can't assume that the rules and laws of the world of your parents will work for the world in 20 years.

So yes, question the status quo, question the establishment, but to question it, you must first know it, accept it and then come up with something better.

In your own life, to make it better, you have to open your eyes and be honest with where you are now, what you're doing and where you want to go.

You can't change anything about yourself or about your world until you are honest and have a high level of awareness of how things actually are now, not how you wish them to be.

As regards all of the "rebelling" you may be doing now, all I will say to you is: **what's the end game here**?

What are you getting out of it?

What is it costing you?

Eventually you will change, but will it be too late?

What needs to happen for you to choose to change right now?

Whose attention do you need to have right now, in order to change?

What feeling or rewards are you looking for that could make you choose to change right now?

Who do you really want to be?

The only reason *they* are giving you a hard time is because *they* care and because *they* don't believe you know what is best for you and *they* are concerned.

And let's face it, if what you're doing is damaging you or people around you in a physical or emotional way, then maybe right now, you don't know what is best for you.

You love to prove people wrong, don't you? So prove them wrong.

Show them that you do know what is best for you.

Show them you do have a plan.

Show them you do respect your body.

Show them you do want to work towards YOUR goals.

Show them that you can commit to things that are important to you.

Show them that some things ARE important to you.

Show them that you do have a set of values and rules that are important to you and are the driving force behind everything you do.

Show them that you do have endless passion and energy and you do want to be "left alone" to do your own thing.

And don't be afraid to ask for help.

One of the ironic things about the coming of age era for people is that they rail on about needing to be different and needing to be individuals.

But if you look around, they all sound the same, dress the same, and have the same hairstyles!

You want to be really brave and courageous? Be yourself, say No once in a while, set some boundaries.

If you can't express to *them* that you do have a plan, that you do have an idea about where you want to go, then is it any wonder that *they* keep getting on your case?

How many of you really think that you're all grown up and can run your own life on your terms, yet still expect your washing and cooking to be done for you?

Your parents and guardians won't always be around to pick up after you, so get a head start on your life now, take control, make choices and choose a direction.

This also applies for married couples. Never ever take your partners role for granted. Do what you can do for yourself and let both parties live their life with freedom and dignity.

This country and indeed the world, its corporations, governments, and everything in it, will be your baby in 20 years.

The world of 20 years time (your world of 20 years time) will be a reflection of you and your peers, based either on a continuation of the values and philosophies of your parents, or based on YOUR values and philosophies.

Which world do you want to inherit, and pass on to the next generation?

So what's it going to be? Are you going to happy enough that "this country is rubbish" speak and join in with every other professional critic and career complainer, or are you going to choose your own path, carve your own destiny and make some choices?

If you are afraid that making one choice will cut away some of your options, there is an old saying in Ireland that "*what's yours won't pass you by*", so don't worry, what is meant for you will come around again, but here, now, each moment, you must make choices and decisions for you and you may be surprised what happens when you do make committed decisions.

As the saying goes, "*when you take one step, God takes one step*".

Again, a reminder of that powerful philosophy –

"Until one is committed, there is hesitancy, the chance to draw back. Concerning all acts of initiative (and creation), there is one elementary truth, the ignorance of which kills countless ideas and splendid plans: that the moment one definitely commits oneself, then Providence moves too. All sorts of things occur to help one that would never otherwise have occurred. A whole stream of events issues from the decision, raising in one's favor all manner of unforeseen incidents and meetings and material assistance, which no man could have dreamed would have come his way. Whatever you can do, or dream you can do, begin it. Boldness has genius, power, and magic in it. Begin it now."

Be a free thinker

One of the most important things you can possibly learn in your life is to be a free thinker. I've hit on this point already in the pages that have preceded but the ability to be a free thinker and to own your own mind, your own thoughts and beliefs is crucial.

Whenever you are faced with opposing opinions or beliefs, take a second to reflect and ask yourself "what do I really believe here?"

Free thinkers are the only thinkers.

The Capacity to Change

This point also cannot be laboured enough. Your capacity to be happy and your capacity to lead a fulfilled and productive life is dependent on your capacity to change.

Why? Because, the world around you is always changing, your body is always changing, nothing stays the same for a moment, and to try to "keep things as they are" means that you step outside the flow of life and basically begin dying as opposed to living.

It's like the water in a stream. As long as the water keeps flowing, it remains healthy and fresh, but if it breaks away into a pool, outside the flow, it gets muddy and stagnant and nothing lives in it.

Always be capable of changing, and always be willing to flow with the currents of life, BUT, do remain conscious of the direction you are choosing.

You Are Unique

In the world to come, I shall not be asked, "Why were you not Moses?" I shall be asked, "Why were you not Zusya?"

- Rabbi Zusya

A famous man once remarked that our purpose in life is to seek our brilliant uniqueness and it was his belief that every single one of us, every single one of the 6.7 billion people in the world are unique and that in seeking and discovering this uniqueness, we therefore lead a life of purpose, discovery and passion.

It was also felt that the best way to follow this journey was to be aware of your passions in life and what really got your blood flowing and brought out the feeling of "love" in your life.

In embracing our uniqueness, as opposed to lamenting how we may not "fit in", we connect with the very best parts of ourselves.

Ironically, it is very often the parts of us that we reject and try to hide and suppress that actually reflect our greatest strengths and talents and instead of denying our shadow (as CG Jung called it), we should shine a light on it, become aware of it and embrace those parts of ourselves that we previously may have not accepted.

The other consequence of being unique is that you came into this world for your own unique purpose, to live your own unique life.

Your parents, guardians and peers have had an important role in protecting you and guiding you to your current "maturity", but **DO NOT FORGET**, that you are absolutely responsible for the choices you make and that ultimately you need to stand over the choices you make.

It is no longer enough for you to leave your decision making privileges in the hands of significant others.

Yes, by all means listen to advice and wisdom (even mine) but ultimately your life is shaped by your choices so become aware of the fact that your choices are your own.

Look upon advice as a stranger giving you money. You can choose to spend it, keep it or pass it on to someone else, but to refuse it out of hand would be foolish.

The people in your life mean well, they wish you well hopefully, but ultimately, much of their advice and counsel comes from their own experience, their own life; shaped through their perspectives in order to meet their needs and avoid their fears.

(What makes my advice a little different is, I don't you know, you can't disappoint me, and there is no expectation, so you are free...)

This will be the case even though they will try their best to be completely impartial at times.

Once you accept this, you will feel yourself growing in stature and in character by acknowledging the fact that:

"I am aware that my decision might be unpopular or might be imperfect but I'm willing to stand by my choice because I know it's the right thing."

That is what is known as integrity.

We often try to remain popular and maintain our status in a group by going along with the group, but in fact, it is by speaking your own mind and standing your ground that you create your own place in the group and in life.

In the beginning, you will of course meet resistance, all change does, such is the nature of homeostasis, inertia and nature itself, but as you continue to assert yourself in a manner that is consistent and based on positive intent, people will respect you for this and more importantly, you will respect yourself as you claim your independence for yourself.

Now, know this, and know it deeply, there is only one you.

There hasn't been one of you before, if there was, there would be no need for you to have been born, but you were born.

There won't be another one of you again, there's no need. You are here now. You are here now.

And now that you are here, what shall you do with your time here?

Your friends and associates have an equally different "profile" and hence have a very different purpose in their life, and hence, can and will make different decisions to you.

They have their own contract in life with themselves, their own path to walk.

Your life and your *inheritance* is the product of generations and choices back through your parents and ancestors, with every lesson being passed down to each new generation.

Your friends have a similarly unique ancestral path of learning, perspective and experience that they must continue to learn from and evolve with.

Each new generation, has a chance, nay, an obligation, to stop for a moment and choose whether to continue the trends of your ancestors or to choose new departures while respecting that what has come before has brought you this far.

As a young rebel, an individual hell bent on being "different" this is good news for you.

You are expected to rebel, and you are expected to question the rules that have been given to you, so that you can choose whether those rules serve you and your generation.

Think of it this way. What sort of society would we live in, if we still lived according to medieval laws[4]? As time changes, people change, we all change and society changes.

---

4   Strangely enough, there are many laws still active in Ireland and the UK which were written in the Middle ages and these laws are still being reviewed.

You are absolutely allowed *and expected* to stop and question the status quo and ask if the rules work anymore.

In 20 years time, your kids will be raised by the laws of the day, and it won't be your parents who will be running the country anymore, you will.

But here's the important point as mentioned before.

It is not enough to simply complain about the current rules and to rebel against every form of authority.

You need to choose new rules that do work for you.

You have inherited much from your parents, who inherited much from their parents.

Some good, some not so good, but every choice was a human choice, made with the best of intentions at the time, given the resources available to them.

It's a real moment of growth and maturity when you look at your parents and realise that, despite their best intentions and efforts, they are imperfect, like us all. There comes that time when you realise, through different eyes, that your parents are humans also, who were once young, have had their pains and trials, and when that moment comes, you can view your parents as friends, not as guardians and not as people whose responsibility it is to provide for you, or indeed choose for you.

So, what will your children inherit from you?

Shall you pass on the mistakes of previous generations to them?

Will you create new mistakes to pass on to them?

Will you simply blame previous generations for how your life turns out?

Or will you stand up and say "this doesn't work, there is a better way."

Will you look at where you came from and choose the next steps?

Will you choose to cease the mistakes that came before and create something better from here on in?

There is no absolute truth, and the truths that apply to your life, must be questioned and reflected upon by you, because although many people will have opinions on what is right or wrong for you, you are the one who must live your truth.

What will you do...?

What will you do today?

"Millions long for immortality who do not know what to do with themselves on a rainy Sunday afternoon."

- Susan Ertz

Stop Pretending

A later section will deal with the importance of being authentic and the value and importance of being self-aware and self-accepting.

One of the effects of the boom years of the Celtic Tiger was the unfortunate loss (temporarily) of our authenticity and humility as a people.

In our consumer driven race, we became competitive but ironically, our competitiveness with each other only made us want to be like everyone else and not like ourselves.

We became a nation of pretenders, trying to fit in and be good enough. We associated our sense of self with these possessions and "achievements."

Our answer to "who am I?" was in the form of "I'm a banker. I'm in IT. I'm in property. I'm an entrepreneur."

Was this all we were? Were we purely defined by our career choice?

Who are you? We lost all connection with our real sense of who we are individually and collectively.

If there is one good thing that can come out of the recession and the loss of much of our wealth is that this has resulted in the dropping of our masques and the revealing of our real selves again.

If I am no longer a banker/property investor/mortgage broker, then what am I? Who am I? Before I became these "careers", who was I? What did I love? What made me unique?

In time, we'll laugh at how we lost ourselves and became these "titles" which we assumed and we'll laugh when we think of all the gadgets and get-rich-quick and get-fit-while-you-sleep products we spent so much money on.

This too shall pass and as the song goes *"freedom's just another word for nothing left to lose."*

With the loss of wealth and material possession so too will many experience a loss and a shedding of old identities, personas and ego-driven beliefs.

It will initially feel unsettling because we have come to identify with all of these false Gods, but let the process unfold and allow the fake skin to be shed and know that what will be left (bankrupt or not) will be the real person who existed before the boom, before the career/position and before the race began, and that's where certainty lies and that's the only foundation upon which you can build your future.

You must get to know yourself, accept yourself, love yourself and be yourself.

Power within You

We are all born with an incredible, almost limitless energy. It's the will to live, the survival instinct, the creative urge, the libido, desire.

Whatever you wish to call it, it's the same force that manifests in artistic creativity, sexual expression, entrepreneurial spirit and musical performance, whatever.

It's also the same basic energy that can result in wars and revolution and romantic arguments.

It's all the same basic driving energy expressed in different ways.

This energy is constantly moving and it constantly needs to move, to grow and expand, that is the nature of this driving force.

It is the nature of evolution, it the nature of growth, learning and transformation.

This energy and this force demands to be expressed in whatever way it can.

This energy lies within you and this energy is already a part of you.

This energy is you and it's up to you how you use it.

Again, the power of choice comes into play.

If this energy and power becomes trapped, misunderstood, stagnant and fails to flow, the effects can be at the very least a sense of frustration, being stuck in a rut, a feeling of dissatisfaction.

At the more extreme ends of the spectrum, you can feel depressed, maybe causing self-harm, harm to others, illness and disease, both psychological and physical.

The amazing thing about this energy is that, though it manifests in different ways, at its root, in its simplest form it is the same force.

Unexpressed artistic passion may manifest as sexual frustration. The energy simply needs to flow.

The choice of the individual is where to point that energy and where to set the destination.

The energy doesn't have to be created, it simply needs to be directed or intended.

That's where our free will comes into play, our choices and our decisions.

One of the easiest ways to tap into that energy is, strange enough, through team sports, where the combination of physical movement and the pursuit of victory make the hormones flow and you tap into something bigger.

Where do you want to direct those energies?

What do you wish to do today? What you do today, creates tomorrow, so don't waste time thinking about what you MIGHT do tomorrow.

This energy, this power is alive now, today, here. Not in the future.

The only moment that exists is Now. This is a scientific fact.

If you had no fear, what would you choose to do?

Put another way... if you had to answer to nobody... if you could not fail... if money was not an issue, what would you choose to do?

Many people are currently unaware of the ability to direct that energy and are simply left with destructive habits, repetitive destructive cycles and illnesses, being stuck, going nowhere. They believe that this is how life is. They believe that this is their lot. They believe that his was how their life was meant to be.

Is that what you believe?

Implosion.

Dying each day, instead of living.

A tectonic struggle between your limitless life-force and the restrictive limitations which have been created by "life".

The irony and the potential tragedy of it all.

What are these beliefs that hold you back?

Where did they come from?

Who did they come from?

What makes these beliefs so carved in stone?

What would happen if you didn't have these limiting beliefs?

What would you do if you were born into the perfect family with endless support, intelligence and money?

What then, would you choose?

I'm betting that you'd sill have the same dreams, but you would now believe that you CAN pursue them.

Here's a thought, pursue them anyway.

"Act as if ye have faith and faith shall be given to you"

Put another way:

"Fake it 'til you make it!"

You'd be surprised how many great business empires were built by a leap of faith which was taken long before all the details were actually in place.

Again, our quote:

"...the moment one definitely commits oneself then Providence moves too. All sorts of things occur to help one that would never otherwise have occurred. A whole stream of events issues from the decision, raising in one's favor all manner of unforeseen incidents and meetings and material assistance, which no man could have dreamed would have come his way."

In particular, teenagers are at that point in their lives where they are on the threshold of leaving their childhood and stepping into the world of adulthood and of "choosing" their direction in life. But are they actually aware of the immense power of creation for their own life which they actually possess?

Are you aware yet, that you do have the freedom and the power?

Are you aware yet that the future belongs to you?

You are leaving the world where you are catered for by your guardians and entering into a world where you can and must make your mark.

This is the bridge.

This journey explains how to take that pure, joyful energy of your childhood and use it as fuel for creating your adult life.

This is about teaching you how to use the exuberance and energy of youth to shape your adult life instead of using adult conventions to shackle and tame your natural youthful energy.

Focus on how to make things a success instead of focusing on how to avoid failure.

This has been one of the biggest mistakes for many who have come before you.

It is the childlike enthusiasm and belief-in-all-things attitude that fuels real success and happiness.

We only make rules and regulations so that 6.7 billion people can get on in anyway although truth be-told, too many rules and regulations muddy the waters and prevent people from simply getting on as fellow human beings.

Don't grow up too fast! Resist the temptation to behave like a grown up and instead, keep a place in your life for innocence, being silly and feeling alive.

Your creative imagination, that same creative imagination that helped history's great inventors, can only be tapped into when you have the curiosity of a child.

The best part of you, the magical and curious part of you is the part that holds the key to your success and happiness.

William Wordsworth had a theory to explain this.

He put it simply:

All children have a sense of wonder; it diminishes as they grow older and are faced with what are called the cares of the world.

Samuel Coleridge said that poets are those who retain that sense of wonder and combine it with the powers of maturity.

I'd go a step further and say that all happy people, all geniuses, all truly successful people are those who retain that sense of wonder and shape it with the lessons and experience of maturity.

Your choice is how and where you wish to direct that energy and apply that sense of wonder. Artistic creation? Engineering creation? Medical Research? Music? Sports?

Create a new energy source? A new brand of politics? A new economic model?

Some people say that there are no inventions left because we have created everything. What utter rubbish.

In a world where there are problems, there are infinite solutions and opportunities.

Until the world becomes truly perfect (good luck with that one), there will never be an end to the need for innovation, wisdom, creativity and a desire to improve.

And who says that our world today has no problems?

Population explosion, food shortages, water scarcity, climate change, crime rates, terrorism etc etc?

Some people see these things as problems, others see them as market sectors.

That is what we need you to be.

That is what we need the land of Saints and Scholars to be.

The visionaries of the future, and having these visions based on a true rock and foundation of awareness of who you are and a real certainty from which you, personally make better choices for you and then collectively, you and your friends make better choices.

With a combination of your various levels of intelligence and with your self-awareness and awareness of and curiosity about the world you live in, there is no limit to what can be achieved.

Every great movement in history began with one person meeting another of like mind, and somewhere, in a room, a discussion arose about something better being possible, about the possibility of tomorrow being better for everyone.

The new leaders.

This is what I am asking of you. Can you be the new Leaders? If you can't, you can be certain that somebody else your age will be, so why not you?

You need to be the ones to take on this challenge, because a problem not solved today multiplies every day after that.

This is your world that you are inheriting.

If you can tap into that energy inside you, and you will, you can pour that energy into any part of your life and energize and infuse it so that you can apply yourself to anything.

Open your mind now to the possibilities for how you can direct your talents, time, resources and energies.

Open your mind now to the possibilities for you helping your country to become a true centre of excellence, guided by the lofty values and ideals that drove the Renaissance and that make you the Saints of today, and match those ideals with the application and endeavour of history's greatest entrepreneurs and creators and give us the Scholars to show the way to our future.

In doing so, you need to take control of your greatest resource, your mind. Your mind controls every part of your life, and there is no aspect of your life that is not directly influenced by your mind.

The degree to which you have dominion over and work with your own mind, dictates how your life will be shaped.

You may or may not be familiar with the epic John Milton poem "Paradise Lost, Part II".

In it there is a quote which sums up the effect of our minds and thoughts on the quality of our life:

"The Mind is its own place, and in itself can make a Hell of Heaven and Heaven of Hell"

Goose-bump Moments

"Let yourself be silently drawn by the stronger pull of what you really love."

- Rumi

I have made and will make reference to choosing, deciding, taking action and creating your lives, and your environment. That is important, that is what being alive is about, creating effect.

A vital ingredient about these activities, whatever activity it is, is that it's what I call a **goose-bump moment.**

You know the kind I'm talking about, those moments when the hair stands on the back of your neck, you feel all tingly and time seems to stand still.

Those moments when you couldn't give a hoot about the world's opinion of you, a feeling of "aah... I really *feel* like me."

Those times when you stop thinking and just experience being.

Different people experience this feeling doing different things.

Playing music, listening to music, singing a song, hearing a favourite song, seeing a random act of kindness, performing a random act of kindness, your first kiss..., remembering your first kiss, scoring a goal, your favourite team scoring a last minute winner, witnessing a natural wonder and much more.

What are your moments of majesty?

They are the simple things in your life, the uncomplicated things you love.

People have the most unique and individual experiences that produce the goose-bump moments but nobody can deny that it's the greatest feeling there is and if only you could bottle it... now there's an idea that will make someone millions someday ☺

Before you go any further, see if you can jot down 10 simple things that you truly love in life, simple things that when you think about them, you get a feeling of happiness. Go on, take 5 minutes and come back to me...

So that's your goal, your compass, your barometer, your tour guide. Whenever you feel those goose-bump moments, you're on the right track.

Search out the goose-bumps, and if you find them. Well actually, it's not even about searching them out.

Just recognise the feeling and stay with it, recognise how it feels, what you were doing when you felt it and know that it will come around again.

That childlike sense of wonder, of magic. It's essential to life, in fact, that feeling is the feeling of life.

When you get that feeling, then whatever you are doing at that moment is the right thing to be doing, so use it as a compass to guide you.

Certainty contains these goose-bump moments.

Keep in mind, that when a joyful experience is shared with others it is multiplied.

It's all about finding your joy and following it.

To put it more accurately however, your challenge is to find joy in whatever you do as far too many people are out there "chasing" that elusive joy. Find the joy in the simplest things and you are well on the way to further happiness.

As an aside, science has connected these "goose bump" feelings with the flow of beneficial hormones and chemicals such as endorphins, and serotonin resulting in a reduction in cortisol and adrenaline which increase the acidity and disease in the body.

So on the plus side, when you have these moments of joy and bliss in your life you are actually enhancing your immune system and fighting infection and disease, whereas if you find that your life is currently void of any joy, you may also find that you are more prone to head colds, flu, irritable bowel syndrome and others.

So, go, seek out and recognise those simple things that give you that buzz, that whoosh, that goose-bump feeling.

An American businessman was at the pier of a small coastal Mexican village when a small boat with just one fisherman docked. Inside the small boat were several large yellow fin tuna. The American complimented the Mexican on the quality of his fish and asked how long it took to catch them. The Mexican replied only a little while. The American then asked why didn't he stay out longer and catch more fish?

The Mexican said he had enough to support his family's immediate needs.

The American then asked, but what do you do with the rest of your time?

The Mexican fisherman said, "I sleep late, fish a little, play with my children, take siesta with my wife, Maria, stroll into the village each evening where I sip wine and play guitar with my amigos, I have a full and busy life, senor."

The American scoffed, "I am a Harvard MBA and could help you. You should spend more time fishing and with the proceeds buy a bigger boat, with the proceeds from the bigger boat you could buy several boats, eventually you would have a fleet of fishing boats. Instead of selling your catch to a middleman you would sell directly to the processor, eventually opening your own cannery. You would control the product, processing and distribution.

You would need to leave this small coastal fishing village and move to Mexico City, then LA and eventually NYC where you will run your expanding enterprise."

The Mexican fisherman asked, "But senor, how long will this all take?"

To which the American replied, "15-20 years."

"But what then, senor?"

The American laughed and said "That's the best part. When the time is right you would announce an IPO and sell your company stock to the public and become very rich, you would make millions."

"Millions, senor? Then what?"

The American said, "Then you would retire. Move to a small coastal fishing village where you would sleep late, fish a little, play with your kids, take siesta with your wife, stroll to the village in the evenings where you could sip wine and play your guitar with your amigos...."

"But, senor, that is what I am doing already..."

Your Purpose

So with this limitless energy available to us and with so much potential in front of us, where do we go, what do we choose to do?

This is where a sense of purpose is important.

As humans we are much more than a collection of bones, tissue, organs and cells.

We are more even than our learned personalities and conditioned responses.

We are more than our emotions.

Each one of you is an individual spirit, with a fingerprint, energy, a gift.

When I use the word spirit, you can take any meaning you want from that.

If it suits you to see that as a religious aspect of you, then that's ok.

If you are not religious, then that's ok too.

If not, you can choose to regard it as your higher consciousness, the real you, whatever feels right for you.

It can even be that goose bump feeling you get when something really amazing happens to you or around you.

The sole purpose of that spirit if you forgive the pun, is expression, joyful simple expression of who you are. It's about the expression of that life energy and focusing it to create your life, thought by thought, choice by choice, action by action.

If you are not expressing who YOU are, then what are you expressing? Whose job are you carrying out? Everybody else is taken, so the only person you can be is you.

The individual means of expression for each may be very different, and indeed are very different.

Ultimately, the purpose of life for each of us is to express that joy and purpose in our lives. Whatever you do, work, play or even rest, do so in a way that is you, that expresses you.

That is why we have beasts of burden to carry out the mundane tasks of carrying our wares.

That is why we invent and create machinery and automated systems to take care of the repetitive, laborious and necessary jobs that we humans find too mind-numbing.

We are not animals, we are not machines. We are evolving, creative, expressive spirits with a deep yearning for expression, joy, discovery and fulfilment.

Your purpose in life is to be you, and to simply enjoy being you.

Realise this, and you will see that even making money can become a very simple task.

The Need to contribute

"Many people have a wrong idea of what constitutes true happiness. It is not attained through self-gratification, but through fidelity to a worthy purpose."

- Helen Keller

An individual is only really a member of a community or society if they are contributing in some way.

You are only contributing if you are interacting and communicating.

Everyone has something to contribute, you know you have, and it is equally vitally important that the individual learn to enjoyably communicate who they are and what they have to offer.

As the legendary Liverpool FC Manager, Bob Paisley[5] once said *"If a player is not interfering with play, then he should be!"*

The same goes for you.

If you are not contributing to your own life or to your environment in some way, or adding value, then you should be! You are a part of your environment and need to be impacting it as much as it impacts you. At the very least, you need to be impacting on your own life, do you not?

---

5   If you don't know who Bob Paisley is, go to the back of the classroom and Google him before feeling very ashamed!

You need to be so bursting full of your own existence and presence that anybody who comes within 10 feet of you can actually feel that brimming energy.

There is no such thing as having nothing to contribute.

There is such a thing as being in the wrong company, being in an environment where you have not learned how to communicate your gifts and contributions, or being in an un-inspiring environment.

There is such a thing as being in an environment where there are just so many obstacles, issues and problems, that any sort of positive outlook seems impossible.

I know this, I've been there, we've all been there.

There is such a thing as being in an unsupportive environment where your gifts have gone undernourished. If that's the case, allow yourself 10 seconds to grieve for what has gone by, and when you're finished, continue on with CHOOSING to create your life.

Take for example, a man named **Victor Frankl** who survived concentrations camps and the holocaust in World War II because he knew that whatever else was happening around him, he had the responsibility for and dominion over his thoughts.

Only he had the power to choose what thoughts he kept in his mind. And that got him through years of hell in the concentration camp.

He made a "Heaven of Hell".

Expression and contribution is essential for the individual and society. This is the new world we live in where your contribution and your service is your ticket into the game. Adding value now, is crucial.

How do you define your value? Simple.

How many problems can you solve for people or help with?

There's your value right there.

In a world full of challenges and problems, lies a goldmine for entrepreneurs and problem solvers.

Find a problem that is annoying you or someone else, and find a solution to it.

Bingo, you now have value.

It is a fact of life and a rule of the mind that what you place your attention on, increases.

No longer will you find yourself wasting valuable time and energy on past failings or worrying about what might go wrong in your life. From now on you're going to find yourself only focusing on the positive things you do want in your life, and as you do you will become aware of the potential positive outcomes from your wiser decisions and the potential negative consequences of your, shall we say, weaker decision and actions.

How you spend your day is how you spend your life, so decide how to spend your day and how to fill your time.

So instead of focusing on "problems", focus on your abilities, use your imagination, and find solutions to any "problem" that pops up and you'll find yourself thinking in a brand new way.

As a bonus, when you begin to think in these expansive ways and when you begin to imagine solutions and better ways to do things, you'll strangely find yourself crossing paths with like minded people, in an almost magical way.

Later on, I'll share a famous and true story about the 100th Monkey experiment, which illustrates this fascinating concept.

A man who lost his axe suspected his neighbour's son of stealing it. To him, as he observed the boy, the way the lad walked, the expression on his face, the manner of his speech - in fact everything about his appearance and behaviour betrayed that he had stolen the axe. Not long afterwards the man found his axe while digging in his cellar. When he saw his neighbour's son again, nothing about the boy's behaviour nor appearance seemed to suggest that he had stolen the axe.

Certainty and Confidence

"Whatever is at the center of our life will be the source of our security, guidance, wisdom, and power."

- Stephen Covey

There is one ingredient which we all strive for in life, in the hope that it makes life easier in every way, and that is confidence.

We all wish for more confidence and often envy those who seem to exude confidence.

In fact, we tend to be suspicious of people who do seem confident.

We say things like:

"If I had more confidence, I would do X,Y and Z"

As a quick exercise, complete this sentence 10 times with different endings:

"If I had more confidence, I would…."

Anything interesting pop up?

Ok, let's continue.

Forget about confidence for now, as it doesn't really mean anything. Confidence doesn't give you control over your real choices.

What people really need is certainty. Certainty is concrete. Certainty is something you can feel, it is measurable. It is power.

Certainty comes from within.

You can claim to be confident about something and at the same time not be certain of it.

For example, you can be confident about winning a football game, but you cannot be certain.

You can be certain however about the effort you will put in, you can be certain about the preparation you will put in and you can be certain that you will at least chase every ball.

Certainty gives you control about the items and tasks you actually can control.

Again, in a world of 6.7 billion people, you can be certain about pretty much nothing outside of yourself. You must build your certainty from within.

Certainty is knowing, not believing.

If you really want to have confidence then re-define it as "knowing with certainty".

Instead of wishing you had confidence in yourself, ask that you can feel a sense of certainty about yourself, knowing who you are, your strengths and weaknesses and feel comfortable with that.

Certainty about yourself is about feeling comfortable within your own skin, warts and all.

That's certainty, that's confidence.

Certainty is a vital part of life. When we lack certainty in ourselves, we seek it outside of ourselves.

We seek certainty in other people, in smoking, in drinking, in drugs, because we lack certainty in ourselves.

The irony is that once we find a feeling of certainty in ourselves, we can use it and apply it everywhere in our lives, no matter what the challenge.

Certainty is like a lighthouse. It is a rock-steady, immovable guide and no matter how strong the winds or no matter how high the waves or no matter how jagged the rocks, the lighthouse remains calm, sturdy, consistent and immovable.

It is like the centre of a wheel. Every other part of the wheel can spin around and around, up and down, but the centre, remains consistent, calm, at peace.

When you develop a sense of real certainty, and because of it, real confidence, you can use this feeling and this state of mind to manage any challenge in your life.

When you have real certainty, it's like knowing that there is always a home fire burning, and always a hot dinner waiting for you, no matter where life's expeditions and adventures take you.

Certainty gives you the confidence to go on these adventures.

Certainty is the inner keep of your castle, where your life is lived, where you have protection and nourishment and joy.

Certainty is your launch pad. Certainty helps you to decide yes or to decide no, depending on the situation.

Certainty is a place of inner power, calm and peace from where you live your life.

Certainty is more than giving you the confidence to be the "real you".

Certainty is about finding out who you are, accepting and liking who you are, and then simply being who you are. From this simple, yet challenging philosophy, your life really has to change for the better and with it, your environment.

Self-acceptance is crucial to certainty. Think about it, if you're always going to be fighting internally with yourself, and refusing to accept yourself, how in God's name can you be surprised if other people don't accept you??

The world learns to treat you by how you treat yourself.

With certainty you can explore and accept any aspect of yourself, because that is who you are.

When the world with all of its chaos spins and spins, day by day, having an inner core of certainty built on your own philosophies, values, beliefs and truths keeps you grounded, secure, calm and focused.

When you have that sense of certainty in yourself, you respect other people more because they are no longer a threat to your certainty because only you can control that inner certainty.

You become less defensive and build better relationships and hence a better life for yourself and others.

Certainty needs to be centred on knowledge and truth, on your deepest inner truths, values and on your philosophies.

Certainty is not about having something, but about being somebody and being capable of doing certain things.

As I've mentioned before, to have more, you must do more and to do more you must be more.

Certainty is that rock, that launch pad from where you do more and by consequence, have more in life.

But no matter how much you have, you always remain mindful, that all you ever truly have, is you, and everything else external is transient and "this also shall pass".

In a following chapter, we will begin to build and reveal the real you. There is no need to create anything here but simply awaken what is already there.

You already have the resources and wisdom inside you, you just need to become aware of it, accept it, and most of all have the certainty to live it, and have no fear about "other people accepting you".

Think about it, again, that 6.7 billion number I mentioned. It makes no sense to seek approval outside of yourself as you'll have a hell of a job getting approval off 6.7 billion people!

Feedback is good, but ultimately, it is your inner certainty that defines who you are and who you will become.

Many people have no idea what their values and philosophies about life truly are. Hence, it is very difficult for them to have certainty, isn't it?

First comes the knowledge and then comes the certainty.

So in a few pages, prepare to meet the real you.

Chunking down for Confidence

Before we move on, a very important point about certainty and confidence is to break down your goal of certainty into small enough chunks so that you can build your confidence up bit by bit but based on blocks of 100% certainty.

It is far more powerful and important to be 100% certain of doing a small thing than being 70% certain of doing a big thing. Baby steps are essential because these baby steps build up experience of success and build your self-esteem.

I'll come back to this point in more strict detail later.

For now, this is the point to take with you:

If there is a task or challenge which you feel less than confident about tackling, break it down into smaller steps and pick one of those steps that you feel total certainty about and perfect each step.

Let's take as an example giving a public speech as this is one of the most common fears on the planet.

Everyone feels nervous to some degree about giving a public presentation, so to minimize the apprehension and uncertainty (uncertainty causes the fear), chunk the task down into manageable tasks such as:

1. Preparing your material

2. Being able to speak in your own bedroom

3. Being able to speak in front of the mirror

4. Speaking into a video camera

5. Speaking to a friend

6. Repeating the speech to a group

So already, you have gone from "public speaking" being the 100% scary goal, to it being only maybe 15% of the overall goal and you can feel much more certain that when you have successfully completed the first 4-5 steps, the last step seems more trivial than manageable.

So, chunk down your goal or challenge to make things achievable and at the end we'll go into this in more detail.

Will the real You please stand up?

The most important opinion you will ever have in your life is the opinion you have of yourself. This is often called your Self Concept and it is the sum total of your beliefs, values, philosophies, learnings and how you ultimately view yourself and the world around you.

How and what you think of yourself will dictate your expectations in life, your standards in life, your values, your behaviours, everything.

Your opinion of yourself shapes your life and will project far beyond any physical behaviour.

The value you place in yourself is far more important than the value you want the world to place in you.

This also raises another issue regarding your self esteem and the satisfaction you feel about who you "believe" you are and who you would like to be. Ideally of course, we would all like the gap between who we believe ourselves to be and who would like to be, to be miniscule.

So, your opinion of you. Who do you think you are? Who do you wish you were?

What makes you unique? What makes you special? What is good about you? What makes you different than the person sitting beside you? Have you ever even considered these questions? How do you value yourself?

It's not about what you have, or what you own.

It's about what and who **you are**.

Think back to our maxim of Be-Do-Have.

You and indeed, we all, need to be clear about who we are, and then what we can do, and only then, will what we have become an obvious consequence and extension of that.

A sense of authenticity is required so that we instinctively know and get a sense of who we really are and that we grow from this centre of certainty and clarity.

Every choice and decision you make in your life is guided by your sense of who you are, whether you do that consciously or unconsciously. Your decisions and choices are dictated by your values, and by your sense of what is important to you, and your underlying priorities in life.

Your choices and decisions are guided by your values and your principles.

Many people are not consciously aware of what their values and principles are. Most people are not consciously aware of what their priorities are.

You can think of it in terms of having your own intrinsic constitution and set of laws if you like, and when you are clear about this constitution and knowing that it is created by you and for you, you know that you can live by this constitution while also recognising and respecting the fact that other people also have their laws which they live by.

We need to become aware of what our true values are, and to become aware of what really works for us. Initially, when you make this discovery, much like any other skill we learn, it may seem a little clumsy at first as we integrate it into our everyday lives. Gradually, however when we become comfortable with these values, beliefs and philosophies, they then can be allowed to return to our unconscious mind, performing a SatNav type function, guiding us away from danger and towards our real destinations.

You're going to see yourself from a completely different angle and you're going to, perhaps for the first time in your life, really get a sense of what it means to be you and what you're about. It is going to mean, initially, changing how you deal with many of your peers and your family.

This is only a settling phase as you find your feet, but what's the alternative?

We all need to discover who we are if we are going to be of any use to the world around us, are we not?

When you are clear about who you are and what you represent, you'll soon realise that everything about you reflects this underlying philosophy and sends a signal to the world.

As you become clearer (in fact it's all about remembering, because it's always been there) about who you really are, and most importantly, accepting who you are, you'll find yourself re-balancing and letting go of old beliefs and habits that were never really yours to begin with and instead you'll begin to connect and re-connect with what was actually closer to your heart.

When you think about your self-concept and your sense of who you are currently, you can realise that your clothes, your car, your friends, the books you read, the websites you visit, your opinions about your world, are all a reflection of who you are and what you represent. In one form or another, who you are, how you behave, the contents of your life are an expression of your current philosophy in life.

Of course, there are many things in your life currently that may represent some old out-dated and redundant philosophies and it may be a good idea for you to perform a bit of a spring clean and bring yourself up to date with yourself.

As an exercise, spend some time later today, looking through your wardrobe, your CD collection and other belongings and ask yourself if they represent who you are and to what degree. It is entirely acceptable to come to a decision that a lot of your old possessions can be sent to a recycling centre or clothes bank.

To allow the new to come in, you must clear out the old.

Your philosophies underpin your beliefs and perspectives on life and in turn influence your decisions and actions in life, so be under no illusion that this is a very real and tangible part of your life.

Conscious Evolution

This is exactly the time in your life when you must take a step back and clarify where you have come from, where your parents came from, your current philosophies and beliefs about yourself and life and really find out if they truly represent how and where you are now in life.

At this point in your life, it is very possible that your opinion of yourself and your beliefs, philosophies, decisions and habits have all been pretty well programmed into you by parents, friends and other environmental influences.

But now is the time to be open to change arriving in some of these areas.

Now is the time for YOU to shape you, instead of being at the mercy of your environment.

It is an accepted fact that people's performance and expectation of themselves is largely shaped and indeed limited by the expectations of the environment and those around them.

You must now break that trend and ensure that you are not overly-influenced by your past programming and by your environment, but that instead you are guided and influenced by your own values, principles and by your own philosophies.

It is time to no longer be unconsciously shaped by your environment but to choose your direction, choose your blueprint and choose your changes.

This is a point of conscious evolution for you.

So, who are you, really? What defines you as a person?

What are your real priorities in life?

What do you love in life and what don't you tolerate in life?

What do you value about yourself?

What influences do you wish to attract in life?

What sort of people do you wish to have around you in life?

What influences do you no longer wish to have in your life?

Your life is shaped by your choices.

Your choices are shaped by your priorities and values.

Now is the time for you to become consciously aware of what those priorities and values are.

Everything you do and say reflects those inner values and priorities.

Every thought, every word, every action reflects this underlying you.

What is sacred to you?

We all need to be very clear about what is sacred to us. What is sacred to you individually and I wonder what is sacred to us as a nation, a society and as a people.

Can it be any surprise that there is often confusion at a national level, when we are not clear and true about what we hold to be most sacred and most dear.

All of us need to know at a personal and a collective level what is sacred to us, where we draw the line. It is this line that then makes it easier for people to deal with us and to know where they stand with us.

It is these sacred items, around which we build our priorities, build our dreams and focus our energies.

A little later, there will be a chapter on your Mission Statement and this point is incredibly important there also. If we do not consciously know what is sacred to us and if we do not cultivate that level of awareness about ourselves, then we are shooting in the dark in terms of knowing what drives us, what motivates us and what is really making us tick.

So what is sacred to you? What would you not compromise on? What really drives you and makes your blood pump? When you know this, you shall know you. Every day can be so much more focused for you, so much clearer when you know what is sacred to you and when you arrange your energies and efforts around that.

Your mission statement in life and inner constitution becomes obvious when you allow yourself to simply be you, if even for one minute.

If you knew you could not fail or if you had no fears, the real you would come shining through.

If you believed that everyone and everything in the world was there to support you, not cheat or hurt you, the real you would become instantly visible.

If you believed you already had all the money you could ever need, the real you with your true talents would immediately step forward.

If there was no such thing as money, how would you get by? What service would you provide in order to get food or shelter?

If the only currency you possessed was your mind, your skills, your abilities, what could you offer the world as your product or service in order to "buy" other goods or services?

Think about this for a while, because when you have an answer to these questions, you will have a real clue as to where your true strengths lie and you will then wake up to the real you, and you will then discover your natural and intrinsic value in the world and once you do, any issues regarding self-esteem or confidence just melt away.

If you could take a holiday from all the "reasons" and "excuses" you tell yourself for not allowing yourself to be the real you, you can remember who you are again.

"*Who*" is wrong with you?

Louise L Hay once said that when people came to her for help, she never asked them "*what* is wrong with you" but "*who* is wrong with you."

All of our fears in life can be distilled down into two basic fears.

Fear 1 – Fear of not being loved

Fear 2 – Fear of not being good enough.

We are conditioned to require love and support and recognition from our parents, peers and guardians and society as a whole.

When all the fear and doubt is put aside for even one minute, then and only then can that real you stand up and be honest with yourself.

It is time to wash away those fears from every aspect of your life.

These fears were fine when you were a baby and you depended upon your parents' attention to survive. But you no longer need that, and also, you no longer need anyone's approval, and what's more, you no longer deserve anyone's criticism.

But you do need a greater awareness of who you are and you do need to take responsibility for you and your choices.

So what's it going to be?

The world is waiting for you to arrive.

I could say "what" is holding you back, but no, the question is "**who** do you believe is holding you back?"

Perhaps the only person holding you back is you?

It's time for you to at least change the perception of being held back and ask yourself:

"If these limitations did not exist, what would I do and who would I be?"

Pause for a moment, and answer this for yourself many times and accept every answer that rises into your mind and you may find yourself remembering moments in your life when you really were you and when you didn't need to get the approval of your mates or anyone else. Everything was perfect, if even for a moment.

In that, quiet simple moment, you become acutely aware of what is really important to you and about you.

Your lesson and task here is simply to make the decision to want to be the real you.

Make the decision to be aware of when you are looking for approval from others.

Make the decision to raise your awareness, accept who you are, and take responsibility for who you are.

Consider the Following

1. **Think of one person who you can't say no to or a situation in the past where you could have said no, but repeatedly didn't.**

    Who are you afraid of disappointing?

2. **What are you afraid of happening if you say no?**

3. **How did they react the last time you said no?**

4. **Put yourself in their shoes and try to imagine why you feel they reacted in that manner?**

**5.   Knowing this, is that a valid reason for you to
       not have the right to say no?**

Growth, progress and improvement require change and
that change must come from within you. This isn't always
easy, but it's always easier than you first imagined.

Answer those questions above, and answer them honestly.
You don't need to tell anyone, and you don't need to
make any global announcement. Just become aware and
change will already have begun for you.

Your right to be magnificent

If you're Irish, then you are well aware of the fact that
you're not allowed to get too big for your boots and that
quite frankly success is only tolerated as long as you don't
become more successful than your neighbour.

I'm not quite sure how this applies in other countries but
I'd imagine there are traces of it everywhere.

The unfortunate thing is that very often the people we
would rely on to support us and help us to achieve our
goals are also the people who can be your biggest obstacles
i.e. friends and family.

Before you pick up the phone and ring them and blame
them for everything, continue reading.

We are all stuck in roles from time to time and we are all
caught in a web of expectation of each other, maintaining
the status quo, and also protecting each other for failure.

When someone close to us begins to "move on", we feel
threatened. Whenever someone close to us seems to be

"changing" or growing, we feel threatened and wonder "is it me" or we feel that they aren't the same person they were.

We can then try to dissuade them, block them or if they do become successful and haven't brought us with them, well aren't they the selfish so-and-so eh?

All part and parcel of being mammals I guess.

My point here is that, even if the people around us are engaged in these dramas as we call them, we don't have to play the game.

First and foremost, at the very least, we have to become familiar with these situations and then, we will at least have the awareness to realise, "well, tough, this is me, and if you won't support me then at least don't block me."

Now, it rarely comes to this, because we end up sabotaging ourselves internally without any external blame being needed.

So as with everything, the work has to be done on ourselves.

Consider the following questions.

1. **What is your greatest talent? Full bragging permission granted.**

2. **How often do you express it?**

3. **Is there anybody who you feel you cannot feel this brilliance around?**

4. Have they ever actually said or done anything to make you feel this way?

5. If so, what did you think when it happened?

6. If not, what's stopping you from doing these things?

7. If these "reasons" did not exist, what would you do?

8. How can your talent be used to help other people?

9. Is there any reason why you should be prevented using your talent?

10. What's more important, using your talent for everyone's good or hiding it to keep people happy?

11. How do you feel about other people who like to talk about how good they are?

12. How often do you congratulate other people sincerely on their triumphs?

13. Do you honestly, honestly believe in your right to be successful and happy?

The answers to these questions will go some way to help you to uncover some of the reasons why you've been hiding your light under a bushel as they say.

Most of the reasons will be internal, yours. Yes, other people may say and do things, but if you let that stop you on your journey through life, that's still your inner obstacle.

Remember, this is your life, you are the lead role.

Your constitution and philosophies

"Those are my principles, if you don't like them, I have others!"

- Groucho Marx

Now, we're going to get you clear about **your** message and who you are.

Become aware of all of the things that you really enjoy in life, that make you feel good, and that are important to you in life.

You don't need to compromise on the things that bring you joy, despite the best opinions of others and the world at large.

The first step to being happy in life is to know what makes you feel happy, just like those goose bump moments I mentioned before.

And every time you feel that connected feeling, it brings you more in touch with who you are and you then find it so natural and easy to accept who you are as you forget what it feels like to hold back those natural feelings of who you are.

For too long, you've held back the real you out of fear that someone may stop loving you, or somebody might get jealous, or that you felt that you might not be good enough.

For too long, you've held back the real you because it may not have "matched" the herd, and that was understandable, but really, you never thought that could continue forever, did you?

So, when is the time to change?

Now of course.

Now is the time to clarify who you are, and to move forward from here, with the sense of certainty we mentioned earlier.

Above all else, do not let fear cripple you or hold you back.

Stay in touch with that sense of who you are and accept that, yes of course you're different, that's the beauty of life, being unique.

You will always have so much in common with other humans, naturally, by default, so don't be at all alarmed or afraid if slight differences and idiosyncrasies appear in you, as otherwise, you'd simply be a clone wouldn't you?

Who wants to be a clone?

Hang on to what makes you unique, even your accent. It's amazing how many people are picking up this TV-Mid-Atlantic accent. Why? Your accent is a part of you and you are far more interesting with it than if you sound like everybody else.

You have a unique ancestry which defines you and it is important that no matter if some aspects of that are in anyway "embarrassing" to you, you accept it as part of you.

And as you continue to accept yourself and your right to be unique, it also becomes easier to accept others and it becomes even easier for others to accept you.

This is one of the simple riddles of life.

If you want something from the world, you give it first.

If you want more patience from life, learn to give it.

If you want more honesty from life, learn to show it.

Whatever value you want to see expressed in the external world, you must learn to live it first.

Again, as Ghandi stated, "you must become the change you want to see in the world".

Every thought, every word, every action, is a projection of who you are. You must and will become, literally, an advertisement, a Times Square, a Piccadilly Circus of your philosophies and values and you will be clear about them and everyone else will see this clarity also.

People will know you better and will know your boundaries and will begin to dance to your tune.

It's as if the world has been waiting for you to arrive, for you to emerge.

If your life feels as if it has been stuck in a rut until now, then that's exactly the reason why.

You haven't arrived yet. You've been holding *you* back. But that's ok, most people have, and most people are waiting for some external authority to give them permission to be themselves.

No, no and no again.

The permission comes from you and nobody else.

When you're holding yourself back, it's like being in a trance and when you are in that trance, the winning lotto numbers could appear to you, all sorts of opportunities could appear and you wouldn't see them.

Until you give yourself permission to be true to yourself, you will feel stuck and will feel trapped.

It really doesn't have to be that way.

And what could be easier than being yourself and what could be easier than expressing the simple values that resonate with who you are.

Everyone lives life by a set of principles and everyone has their own unique list of principles, even if they are not explicitly aware of what they are, and you can now become more aware of what your unique principles are.

You do not need to belong to a herd. The aim of your life is to become wonderfully unique, because when you do, and when you really learn your true value, and your abilities, you can then choose to contribute them and collaborate with other unique and brilliant individuals in creating magnificent things for you and for the world.

You can maybe imagine yourself sitting at a desk like Leonardo Da Vinci in candlelight, with a big quill and a pot of ink and you can imagine yourself drafting up your constitution for yourself.

And as you imagine this you can go a step further and imagine choosing your values for your life, the ones that work for you and your life.

Values and principles that define what you, on one hand, truly love in life, and on the other hand define what you do not tolerate in life. A list of the does and don'ts that work for you.

What are your absolute must haves in life and what are your absolute no-nos in life?

Think back to the Goose bump moments you looked at earlier.

List 10 simple things that you love in life.

What simple things, throughout your life, give you the greatest joy, the greatest sense of freedom?

What simple activities or moments in life make you feel truly alive and have left you with vivid, colourful living memories that are as real now as they were then?

It has been said that life is all about those moments when you felt happy and I truly believe that. There was no perfect day, week, year or decade. There are always challenges.

But there are also always moments, pure moments when you wished you could stop the clock and milk that moment for all it was worth. Remember these moments. What was it about these moments that make you want to shed tears of joy?

What is it about these moments that bring up those goose-bumps?

What have your friends always said was different about you?

What have you always felt was unique about you?

If you were truly the King or Queen of an ideal land, what would be the most important values and principles you would rule by? How would you rule your kingdom?

Perhaps honesty is important to you. Perhaps gratitude is important to you. Forgiveness, patience, kindness, passion, excitement, humour perhaps.

You love to laugh, of course. If you don't enjoy laughter, then there is a deeper need to stop and ask yourself where has life brought you.

As you ask yourself these simple questions and remain open to the answers coming to you in various forms, even without you doing anything, you will find that your subconscious mind is already gently re-arranging your mental and emotional furniture to reflect these values and priorities to ensure that your thoughts, words, and actions are in line and congruent with the values you have chosen and which have chosen you.

It is as if your subconscious mind is installing signposts for you.

And every time you make a decision or choose a direction in life, your subconscious mind checks these signpost, consults your constitution, and you naturally find yourself travelling along the right road always.

But as an exercise now, actually write down these moments, memories and values that are important to you, the must haves and the building blocks that a happy life must have for you. There are no limits here and now, so let it flow.

As a corollary now, also think about the times in your life, when you have gotten angry over something, when you witnessed someone's behaviour that really hit you at your core and that you would never tolerate or allow yourself to do or most importantly times when you yourself have violated your own values and rules.

This is also, just as important. This defines your standards for yourself, and by having these clear standards and rules for your own life, you give it real shape and discipline and you can really begin to trust yourself and then go with your instincts.

This is important because if you do not have your own clear standards at a conscious level, then when you do violate them, they are still being violated at a deeper level and this causes all sorts of confusion and guilt that you can't put your finger on.

Become clear about these limits for you.

It's very easy for people to write down 10 values that they believe we should have and we believe we do have.

It is however far more productive if you sit back for a second and be honest, and ask yourself about those times when you clearly broke your own rules and violated your own values. Those are the moments that give rise to your guilt on the inside and wrong directions on the outside.

So take a moment now, to make a little confession to yourself about the times in your life when you did those things which, if given a second chance, you would not do again.

And when you've done that, now make a promise to yourself, update your constitution to indicate that you will do your very best to not do it again!

The reason? Well, insanity has been defined as doing the same thing over and over again and expecting different results. If it ended in disaster the last time, chances are it will the next time, so choose a new action and a new law for yourself and make a decision to take baby steps to fix it for you.

Your Philosophy and Values

So what is the point of all this?

Well, if I told you about a friend of mine called John, who earned €1,000,000 a year, owned 4 houses and drove a Porsche, and told you nothing else, would you feel like you knew John?

Would you let John babysit your kids? Would you trust John?

On the other hand, if I listed out all of John's values (from the list above), and also John's absolute no-nos in life, then would you say you knew John?

I'd bet the answer is yes to the second one?

When you know someone's values, philosophies and standards in life, even without meeting them, you already have a deep insight into them as a person.

So, by you being absolutely clear about your philosophies and values in life, you now know yourself better.

And what does that give you?

Certainty.

It gives you certainty about who you are and what is important to you.

It allows you to choose your battles in life.

It allows you to apply your focus in life. Nobody can be all things to all men. There are only 24 hours in the day, 8 of which, on average, are spent sleeping, so by knowing your values, philosophies, and priorities in life, you can begin to spend your precious time focusing on what is really important to you, and as you get older, you will really learn how important that is.

So, by now you should have some idea of your philosophies on life, what you believe life should be to you and how you believe a worthy life should be lived. If your list is still a bit short, don't worry because this is now a process which has been kicked off and once your unconscious mind goes on a search like it is now, it keeps going until it finishes, so you're going to find yourself thinking about this every hour or so until you are completely finished.

Living Your Values

If you are very aware of your values in life and what is really important to you, BUT, you find that you don't act on them or indeed shy away from them in everyday life, this can give rise to a great deal of internal conflict, guilt, anger and much more.

If you find yourself breaking your own rules, you can end up getting really over-the top angry with yourself and indeed others over other un-related issues.

An important point to mention is that people who do not accept their own perceived faults and failing in themselves, end up projecting them onto others.

It is really important that you take baby steps in practicing your own preaching, oh and also to not preach!

Learn to take baby steps, first in easy situations, to practice your own values and your own code of ethics and code of honour.

Strive for the expectation that your inner values and external reality are as close and with as little divergence as possible. Aim for being really true to yourself as a person.

One of the great skills for this is in saying No, and setting boundaries, and we'll get to that later.

It's about becoming aware of what is really important to you, what is sacred, what do you value?

But for now, take a moment to go through your values and your philosophies in life and imagine every day scenarios where they may be challenged or you may have an opportunity to express them.

Become conscious of situations in your own life, where you just may not be living up to your own standards and values for one reason or another.

We all have our own song to sing and it is a real waste when we hide ours light under a bushel or betray ourselves in order to remain one of the herd.

Be true to who you really are

"Once upon a time, while walking through the forest, a man found a young eagle. He took it home and put it in his barnyard where it soon learned to eat chicken feed and to behave as chickens behave.

One day, a naturalist, who was passing by, inquired of the owner why it was that an eagle, the king of all birds, should be confined to live in a barnyard with the chickens.

"Since I have given it chicken feed and trained it to be a chicken, it has never learned to fly," replied the owner. "It behaves as chickens behave, so it is no longer an eagle."

"Still," insisted the naturalist, "it has the heart of an eagle and can surely be taught to fly."

After talking it over, the two men agreed to find out whether this was possible. Gently the naturalist took the eagle in his arms and said, "You belong to the sky and not to the earth. Stretch forth your wings and fly." The eagle, however, was confused; he did not know who he was, and seeing the chickens eating their food, he jumped down to be with them again.

Undismayed, the naturalist took the eagle, on the following day, up on the roof of the house, and urged him again, saying, "You are an eagle. Stretch forth your wings and fly." But the eagle was afraid of his unknown self and the world and jumped down once more for the chicken feed.

On the third day the naturalist rose early and took the eagle out of the barnyard to a high mountain. There, he held the king of birds high above him and encouraged him again, saying, "You are an eagle. You belong to the sky as well as to the earth. Stretch forth your wings now, and fly."

The eagle looked around, back towards the barnyard and up to the sky. Still he did not fly. Then the naturalist lifted him straight towards the sun and it happened that the eagle began to tremble, slowly he stretched his wings. At last, with a triumphant cry, he soared away into the heavens.

It may be that the eagle still remembers the chickens with nostalgia; it may even be that he occasionally revisits the barnyard. But as far as anyone knows, he has never returned to lead a life of a chicken. He was an eagle though he had been kept and tamed as a chicken.

Never let anybody convince you that you are someone other than yourself. Never seek verification from outside of you. Be open to feedback and advice but always make sure that the voice that comes from inside you is louder than the voices that you hear outside.

Never lie to yourself to make it easier to fit in or to make it easier for others to be around you. You are who you are for a reason and no matter how long you pretend to be somebody else, the truth will always be welling up inside until someday it escapes. Don't waste time, make that moment of revelation today.

The Power of No, Setting your Boundaries

"I run me and you run you"

It would be easy to think that everything you have read so far has given you the impression that you can simply go out and do what you want with no consideration for the consequences of your actions. You are the lead role in your life after all aren't you?

Yes, but as the old Wiccan creed goes *"And it harm none, do as thou wilt"*. In other words, yes, be free, be bold to do what you wish, AS LONG as you don't cause harm to others.

This doesn't mean tip-toeing around, walking on egg-shells, holding back your real self for fear of upsetting the world around you or offending anyone.

As Buddha once said, "be wisely selfish", ensure that your decisions and choices are for your highest good. If they are, then they are more likely to be beneficial to those around you also.

It's also worth keeping in mind that for someone to be offended or to take offence, it takes two parties. One to cause the offence and one to choose to be offended.

So there is also a very clear difference between DOING bad things to people and people indirectly deciding to be annoyed or hurt by your actions or behaviours.

The difference lies in the word "Intention". Very simple.

When performing any act, you simply ask yourself "what was my intention?"

If it was to cause hurt or cause offence, then yes my friend, you have transgressed, you have injured.

On the other hand if your intention was to pursue something of interest for good reason, and somebody indirectly felt aggrieved, then be slow to feel guilt and be brave and keep your intention in mind and let the storm pass.

Invasion of Boundaries

Every day, with 6.7 billion people milling around trying to meet their needs, it's obvious there are going to be clashes of boundaries, values, needs, resources and more.

It is essential, really essential, for you to be aware of your boundaries, of where your kingdom ends and your neighbour's begins. You must become aware of how it feels when your boundary has been over-stepped, and you must also become aware of when you yourself leave your domain and invade another's for whatever reason.

In an earlier section, you gained a fresh and unique insight into your concept of you and who you are, why you are here and what you stand for, what defines you

This chapter builds on this and looks to establish the concept of boundaries and the right of the individual to say "No", and direct the course of their life.

The values, chosen by you, become an inherent part of who you are, guiding your every thought, word and action in an instinctive way.

You also learn about the subconscious mechanisms of fear and motivation which guide your every choice and habit.

You are presented with the simple truth that you and you alone are ultimately responsible for your choices and despite the pressures from friends or family to conform to expectations, that it is your right to make the decisions which are right for you and your life.

This chapter is about your acceptance and expression of the unique self that you now know yourself to be.

The Power of No

There is a word that is very small, easy to pronounce, but very often very difficult to say.

That word is "no".

There have been many times in your life when you felt that "no" was the right thing to say in a given situation, but for one reason or another, you said "yes".

We've all done it, I know I have many times and you have too.

Whether it is because you fear that somebody would stop loving you or desert you if you said "no" or for whatever reason, we often choose the apparently easier option of saying "yes".

Of course, you often end up feeling a sense of regret later thinking "I should have said no, damn it!"

For whatever reason, you feel that you have given away control of your life for those few moments.

It can be a difficult thing to say and can also be a difficult thing to hear. We don't like hearing the word "no".

It seems to be demonised and loaded with so much emotion and negativity that when we hear the word "no", we can feel rejected, spurned, deflated and demoralised.

But why is this the case, and why should it be the case?

Everyone has the right to say no, just as everyone has the right to choose what is best for their life.

Very often, saying "no" should be as easy as politely refusing sugar in your coffee.

It's about the idea of independence, boundaries and about respecting both your own boundaries and those of others.

By understanding that everyone has their own unique path to follow, and you do too, you will understand that when somebody says "no", it is more often than not a "no" **from them** as opposed to a "no" **to you**.

Everybody, and I mean everybody, is on their own independent journey through life. Very often these independent paths cross, resulting in relationships and exchanges in varying degrees of depth, commitment, duration and purpose.

Regardless of these, everybody is still on his or her own path. If two paths seem to coincide, fantastic. They are still two paths.

The main lesson I'd like you to take from this chapter is this:

When you are being true to yourself and following your instincts, you have full power to say yes and no when you feel the need. You don't lose by saying no, and the things and people you love, do not disappear from your life when you say no, unless you choose.

It's a case of live and let live. When you say No to someone else, you are merely saying Yes to you.

As Tim Gallwey once wrote: "*Other people can have an opinion on how you run your life, but they don't have to have a casting vote*".

When do you say no?

In the last chapter, you learned about your values, principles and constitution. I cannot stress enough how important that exercise was and is.

Your values, principles and constitution are your signposts in life. They are your guide when to say yes and no to things.

If you encounter a situation or a choice that goes against a core principle, do you say yes or no? In your daily life you will meet numerous opportunities to express who you are and what you are. These are the baby steps that define you and that demand courage from you.

Every time you say yes or no and make a decision, you are creating a habit within your mind and what might seem like a harmless "ah, yeah, go on" now could be the straw that breaks the camels back and creates an unconscious habit that sets up as a squatter in your mind and quietly takes over your life.

We'll come back to habits again in a later chapter.

A great deal of this principle is based, not on the concept of WHAT you do, but WHY you do it.

Take for example, on a Friday night, you spend it with your girlfriend or boyfriend.

Case 1 is that you do so, because you love them and love spending time with them, and feel happy doing so.

Case 2 is because you felt that if you didn't spend time with them, they might be angry with you, or might leave you or love you less, or there'll be an argument.

It's not the WHAT, it's the WHY.

Let's take a second example.

You are with a bunch of your friends, they are smoking for the first time and they offer you one.

Case 1 – You know exactly what smoking does for you. Cancer, yellow fingers, yellow teeth, bad breath, etc…

Case 2 – You feel that people will call you boring if you say no.

Every time you say yes or no, you alter the course of your life, maybe a little, maybe a lot. Every time you say yes or no, you are making a statement about you and your defined boundaries.

You are making a statement that says "***these are the rules by which I live my life. Now that you know these rules you know what to expect from me.***"

Make a statement about you. Make a statement about your life and what you stand for.

It is **your** life.

When you say Yes or No for the right reasons, i.e. according to your core values, life will work in your favour and you'll create positive mental habits and expectations of success for yourself and your self-esteem automatically increases.

It is true, at certain times, that it may feel that you're missing out on a short term gratification, but if you are true to yourself, the significance of that short term gain will fade away when compared to the growing sense of self which you are building and in the long run you can have tons more "fun" than those fleeting moments of weakness would ever have brought you.

Boundaries

As an individual staking your claim in the world, it can often feel that your needs aren't being met, that your rights aren't being respected.

It can feel like your boundaries aren't being respected and that the world isn't listening to you.

How do you know they aren't?

Are you fully aware of what your boundaries are and where they lie?

If you are not fully aware, how are other people supposed to know?

If you are not fully aware of the instruction manual for your life, how can others know?

So, step 1. Become aware of the rules of your life. Again it's back to your constitution. Your mission statement. That is the user manual for your life.

Step 2. Bit by bit, implement and express those values. Learn when to say Yes and No.

Every thought, every word and every action, guided by your mission statement. You won't need to need go out looking for situations to implement them or try to make a statement.

Life will provide you with enough wonderful opportunities to make choices and decisions and you'll find that by taking advantage of these, bit by bit, you can get a tremendous sense of achievement by making even small conscious choices with your values in mind.

And the important point is: **THEY ARE YOUR VALUES!**

In the beginning, it may feel as if you're possibly risking losing friends as a result of saying no, but in effect what you're doing is clearing out old debris and setting new boundaries.

All you are doing is making the rules of the game clear and if people want to continue playing, all the better.

The result of this is that you will actually then attract the correct people and situations into your life.

You will find that you will naturally gravitate towards like-minded people.

You will find that you will meet new people who have important things to exchange with you.

You will find that people who you thought you knew well will have the new found courage to show you a deeper side of them.

Your relationships will deepen, become richer and you will begin to operate and to exist on a much richer and deeper level.

You will attract people and situations into your life which "agree" with your values.

They won't necessarily be people who agree with everything you say in content, but they will be people who agree with and respect your right to say it.

So, be the first to make the move. Become your own business card. Become your own brochure. Advertise who you are and what you stand for.

Make it clear what you stand for, the things you tolerate and the things you do not.

Respect other people's choices to choose their own path but most importantly always respect yours to follow your own path.

You are not seeking to dictate to others how they should behave. You are merely making it clear that you have certain principles that you yourself follow.

Very often, it can seem as if some people in your life exist only to antagonise, infuriate or simply annoy you.

Perhaps. But consider this. Subconsciously, these people have chosen to antagonise and annoy you. They chose you. They are expecting a response from you. So long as they keep getting the same response from you, they will continue to behave in the same way.

Consider the possibility that they are subconsciously looking for you to step up to the plate, to make a statement, to lead.

These people have seen something in you that they are trying to provoke into action.

I promise you, if you become your own best advertisement and say "yes" and "no" according who you are, you will attract the life that you do want.

Self-Regulation

It's a fact of life that is you don't establish your own boundaries and regulate your own behaviour, that others will gladly do it for you!

You may know somebody who was a real party animal in their youth and who ended up marrying a more controlling partner to help balance them.

If you are from a farming background, you know how important it is to correctly fence in your animals so as to prevent them from straying onto your neighbours lands.

I'm not saying animals cannot roam free, of course they can. Just make sure that your "animals" do not harm you or others!

You have the right and the responsibility to establish your own well-defined boundaries.

Once you have established them and are clear and consistent about them, people know where they stand with you and apart from feeling more at ease in your company they can begin to respect your boundaries.

Self-Regulation is your first step to self-determination.

Discipline creates freedom.

Acknowledging Other Peoples Rights

We are all aware of the ability of the Irish to cut down our own heroes. "That fella Bono is only a so-and-so". We love to begrudge, we hate to applaud. We'll support each other only as long we don't try to pass each other out.

We seem to be a very competitive nation in many of the wrong ways. Throughout history, we fought battles against each other because we all wanted to be High King and then we invited the Normans in just because we didn't want "the fella next door" to be King. Nice one lads!

We were happier to have a Norman King than to have our neighbour be King.

Begrudging gets you nowhere. Take that as a rule of law.

It can be great fun sitting around bitching about people but it gets you nowhere.

If you begrudge someone winning money, what you are in a sense telling yourself is "it is wrong to have money". If you have this belief that it is wrong to have money, you will live your life wasting money, losing money and subconsciously avoiding money. Fact.

So, if you wish to attract goodness into your life, you have to believe that attracting such luck, goodness and abundance is a very good thing.

You must have the belief that luck, goodness and abundance is a good thing, plain and simple.

If everyone in the world is a millionaire, you are a millionaire.

If everyone in the world is madly in love with the partner of their dreams and enjoying an amazing sex-life, you are madly in love with the partner of your dreams and enjoying an amazing sex-life!

The easiest way to fill your day with happiness and luck is to applaud and congratulate others on theirs. If you can share in other people's good fortune, you're lifting your own mood and multiplying the opportunity to be happy.

So, put an end to begrudging, it gets you nowhere and only serves to keep you in a rut.

Competing for good luck, or competing for fortune is like competing for oxygen. There is more than enough to go around.

So, start to compliment each other in a warm and sincere manner. Start to congratulate each other and you will notice a seismic shift in your own happiness and satisfaction.

And remember, we're all trying to get by on this planet, so live and let live as much as possible.

Your Daily Habits

"How you spend your day is how you spend your life"

Jim Rohn

Your life can only change, and indeed is guaranteed to change if you first of all begin to "think" differently and challenge old beliefs.

But it is extra important then to change your daily actions, your habits, because you only affect your external life through action and the re-programming of your habits.

We touched briefly upon actions and the notion of creating habits in previous sections but let's just bring them together briefly here for an important, simple and powerful exercise.

How many things do you do every day that are unconscious and habitual? There are many good things you do, such as, when you wake up you go straight for your toothbrush. Another one is getting dressed before you walk out the front door. I find that habit really useful!

Habits are important. Habits take control of repeated actions away from our conscious mind and pass them over to our unconscious mind. The reason for this is that our conscious mind has limited capacity and we need it for dealing with the outside world and processing our senses i.e. living.

Our unconscious mind however, is a vast, perhaps infinite storehouse of our habits and routines, good and bad, which are invoked and executed moment by moment every day.

When we learn something new, such as driving, we begin by being very conscious and clumsy and having to check mirrors, seatbelt, clutch, gearstick etc and we can feel as if we'll never get beyond this initial phase.

However, with practice and repetition, we get to a stage where it's all done unconsciously and you drive on auto-pilot quite safely.

Such is the power of habits and the power of your unconscious mind.

Your life is a collection of habits. Your life is shaped by your daily habits and your life will only improve and grow with improved habits.

Up to this point in your life, you might very well have some old habits that you picked up when you were as young as 5 or 6. Those habits served you well back then, but from time to time, just like with your clothes, you need to take an inventory of your habits and throw out what you no longer need and bring in what you do.

Again, to stress the point, how you spend your day is how you live your life and if you keep doing what you used to do, your life will not grow, but remain a series of repeated and predictable cycles. And therein lies the reason we resist change. Predictability, no matter how good or bad can provide certainty, but don't let it fool you.

It is those repeated, daily almost unnoticed actions that shape your life without you even knowing it.

The question for you is have you fallen asleep at the wheel or are you consciously aware of the actions, habits and routines that fill your day?

All the talent and potential in the world means nothing without regular, daily application of effort. The daily application of actions, disciplined conscious actions has more impact on your success in life than any God-given gifts or talents that you believe you have.

Taking an inventory of your Daily Habits

So how are you currently living your life? How do you currently spend your day?

What are the habitual actions you take between waking up and heading out your front door? Have you ever really though about it?

Habits not only include what you do but how you think and how you feel.

If your reaction to somebody who always "annoys you" is to get angry, lose self control and either get into an argument or get into an internal angry spiral, that's also a habit.

When your phone rings and it's your girlfriend/boyfriend or one of your parents and instead of being happy to take the call, you mutter something like "what do they want this time?", that's also a habit.

How do you spend the first hour after you get back home from either work or school? That's also a habit.

Roy Keane once remarked that it's the 1,000 tiny things you do in a game that decide whether you win or lose that game, and not the headline moments.

Every day, you spend minutes and hours working on auto-pilot, thinking old thoughts, executing old habits as the days disappear.

Creating new habits requires that you look at every moment as an opportunity to choose. Creating new habits requires that you use your mind in a more productive way.

Creating new habits requires that you choose to say goodbye to old habits, old ways of thinking and living that no longer serve any purpose in your life.

So starting now, get out a pen and paper and jot down all of those tiny habits that make up the minutes and hours of your day, because it is those tiny habits and baby steps that are continuously shaping your life.

You own your life, you own your thoughts and you are the Lead Role. Nobody else can do this for you.

If you find yourself, right now, thinking, "ah, I'll do it later", that's a habit and a very dangerous one called procrastination! If you tend to procrastinate, then do yourself a favour now and postpone procrastinating for an hour or two.

Again, this is your life, nobody else's, so who or what are you waiting for to do it for you?

As the old adage goes, when you take one step, God takes one step.

Start writing, and start being honest with yourself about those minutes and hours you spend on little habits that no longer serve you.

One of the reasons this is so important is because if you asked somebody why they didn't set some goal for themselves or achieve something, one of the first answers often is "I didn't have the time".

You own your time.

How much time did you spend eating today?

How much time did you spend watching TV?

How much time did you spend rechecking your email?

How much time did you spend on Bebo or Facebook?

How much time did you spend sending SMSs?

It all comes down to, are you merely filling your time and spending time or are you investing your time for yourself.

Be honest and become aware of how you spend your time, because again it is your time, your life.

There will be a full chapter later on Goal Setting and creating new habits for yourself, but here are a few simple principles regarding focusing your mind to create new habits.

Creating new habits

It is in the nature of that storehouse of your habits, your unconscious mind, that it doesn't handle negatives, it strips out the negative and acts on the positive verb or command.

Let me give you an example.

If I ask you to NOT think of a pink elephant, you WILL think of a pink elephant. This is because it ignores the NOT and simply acts on the "think" command.

Similarly, if you are playing golf and you have a 5 foot putt and you are repeatedly telling yourself, "I hope I don't miss this putt", your unconscious strips out the "DON'T" portion and only hears the HOPE and MISS part and you, as expected go on and miss your putt.

The solution to all of this, and a point we will cover in great detail in a later chapter on Goal Setting, is to always focus on the positive and always focus on what you DO want. So, in the golfing example, you tell yourself "I will make this putt".

In relation to our discussion on habits, the relevance of this point is that the way you break an old habit, is to replace it with a new habit.

Yes, there are techniques we use in Hypnotherapy and NLP to actively break up old habits, but that is only one leg of the stool.

It is also essential to create a new habit to replace the old one.

If you do not, you are left with a void, a vacuum and that's possibly more useless to you than the old habit.

Take the old classic. My father always said "once you sit in the sofa you're done!"

You know the scenario, you have all the best of intentions in the world, but once you sit down, getting back up is as difficult as facing a marathon and before you know it, 4 hours have passed and there is still nothing really worth watching on TV.

So, what's the solution?

First of all, from your inventory in the previous section, you are aware of the fact that vegging out in front of the TV is one of your long-term unproductive habits. That's step one, awareness.

Step two involves "ok, what do I want to do instead?" In other words, what new habit do I want to develop instead?

As easy and simple as this may seem, it's actually a huge stumbling block for people.

What do you want to do? What do you want?

Again, the bigger question regarding "what do you want" will be looked at in that later chapter on Goal Setting but for now, in relation to habits, the point is, you must identify a clear habit that you do want to create in order to replace the old habit AND overcome the inertia that has been re-enforced over many years.

Inertia can be very difficult to overcome. Your subconscious mind has a habit in place that it believes works just fine for you. If you want to replace this habit you're going to have to make sure you do it right.

So step 1, you need clarity. What exactly is this habit going to be? Go outside and read a book? Join a sports club? Go for a run? Go for a walk?

Step 2, you need to have a desire for this new habit. This is achieved by recognising the benefits of the new habit. The new habit needs to have benefits for you. Does it make you feel good? Does it help you lose weight? Does it help you to become more confident? Will it help you pass an exam or get a job?

Identify a clear benefit you will get from starting this new habit, one that clearly outweighs any perceived benefit you may have gotten from your old habit.

Step 3, accept the fact that you are human, you are imperfect and that initially, you will slip up with your habit. Discipline your disappointment and avoid ditching the new habit after a slip up. New habits take approximately 3-4 weeks of consistent repetition and practice to become an auto-pilot habit. So go easy on yourself and give yourself a break.

Step 4, give yourself a reward for the new habit. It's that simple, identify a reward you will give yourself by completing this new habit.

I read in one Health magazine that a man motivated himself to lose 7 stone in fat over a year and get in great shape by rewarding himself with a single bottle of

Guinness after completing each 1.5 hour gym workout. This was his little reward which made the gym vs TV contest fun.

And no, it wasn't me ☺

The main learning point from this section is, don't simply try to "give" up a habit without starting a new one. It is in the nature of your subconscious mind to fill that gap with something, so by not creating a new attractive habit, it will either revert to the old habit or pick a worse one itself.

Go easy on yourself

As a final learning point here, one of the most important things you can do is to give yourself a break, go easy on yourself.

By all means set lofty but realistic expectations for yourself, motivate yourself to succeed and give it 100%.

But if and when you do have human failings from time to time, learn from your mistake, don't allow guilt or self-loathing to creep in, dust yourself down and keep going.

As mentioned in another section, persistence is more important than talent or potential.

Discipline that disappointment.

Whenever you hear yourself using the words "you should, you shouldn't, you can't" or other limiting and negative phrases, take a quick rain-check and question this voice. Don't assume that this commanding voice in your mind is always right.

One of the interesting reasons for this is that, when you have those moments of self-loathing, regret and guilt, very often that voice you hear in your head, giving you a hard time, is not even your voice...

I'll leave that thought with you and remind you that you are the King and Queen of your mind and if you have somebody else's voice in there giving you a hard time, it's time to say "thanks for everything up to now but we can't have two bosses, cya!"

Your Powerful Mind

"The Mind is its own place and in itself can make a Hell of Heaven and a Heaven of Hell"

- John Milton

Your Mind is your absolute most powerful resource as you journey through life.

To not be aware of the inherent power of your mind and of the responsibilities regarding its use is as dangerous as drink-driving or carrying a loaded gun without the safety on.

Your mind can be your best friend but can also lead you down dangerous roads if you don't master it.

Every single aspect of your life is directly influenced by your mind, so cultivate it, work with it, and use it wisely.

Everybody should have a users' manual for how their mind works and the effect which their thoughts have on their life.

You can consider this *your* manual, lucky you eh?

Quite literally, your mind and your thoughts determine how you see the world around you and determine your reaction to your world.

How you see the world around you is precisely how the world will be for you.

Albert Einstein once said that the most important decision that we can make in life is deciding whether

we live in a helpful and kind universe or an unkind one.

Your thoughts create your world. Your thoughts directly impact and influence how you exist in the world and therefore the world that you experience.

If you decide that school sucks, work sucks, life sucks and that life is difficult, then I promise you, these beliefs will be true for you.

If on the other hand you decide that school is to be enjoyed, life is to be enjoyed and that you will lead a healthy and happy life, then that too will manifest for you.

So, the only person in the world who has the power and the responsibility to shape and choose your thoughts is you. The only person, who has the power and the responsibility to decide whether in your mind is Heaven or Hell, is you.

From the outset, I want you to take a leap of faith with me.

Instead of you believing that your thoughts are a result of what happens in the world around you, from here on in, be open to the idea that what happens in the immediate world around you is to a great extent a result of your thoughts, a case of as within, so without.

You already know this from the example where if you're in a crappy mood the world looks to be a horrible place but when you're in a great mood the world all of a sudden is a wonderful place and the only thing that has changed is your mood!

Like the classic example, you fancy someone but you start thinking they don't fancy you? So you walk around, down in the dumps, feeling like the world is a horrible place and then…beep beep…you receive a text from the object of your affection and then it's all birds singing, sun is shining and the world is wonderful again!

We've all been there… Even Shakespeare wrote a sonnet about it! (As an exercise, go and see if you can pick out which one!)

Once you become master of your own mind, you become master of your own life.

Becoming the master of your own mind involves achieving clarity about what you want, having the techniques and presence to focus on what you want and having the discipline to then execute actions accordingly.

When you are master of your own mind, you then get to choose your actions in life as well as your reaction to the things you encounter in life in every area of life.

When you are master of your own mind, you can achieve almost anything. Your mind is infinitely more powerful than any computer in the world, any machine, any space ship, and any invention. It will never be surpassed in its capability and its power.

When you are master of your own mind, you don't need anything else because you can produce the happiness and contentment and sense of certainty that the rest of the world goes out and spends a fortune on e.g. drink, drugs, diet pills, designer clothes etc.

People buy these things in excess because they "make them feel good", and make them feel complete, for now…

When you are master of your own mind, you have control over your world, over your thoughts, your actions and behaviours.

So before we embark on exploring the power of your mind, choose now to accept and take control of your mind and to be truly independent of the good opinion of others.

As I mentioned earlier, in your own mind, you are King, you are Queen. You are lord and lady. You are the boss. So now that you are the boss of your own mind are you going to choose to dump toxic waste all over it, or are you going to protect it nurture it and cultivate it for your own good and for your future?

A Danish Philosopher called Soren Kierkegaard once remarked:

"A man who wishes to keep a nice garden does not reserve a space for weeds"

This is your challenge for this chapter. Your mind is yours, nobody else's. Only you have control over what takes place in your mind, so are you going to grow weeds or are you going to turn your mind into a wonderland of creation and innovation?

In our evolutionary quest for growth and discovery, we have been to outer space but it seems the next frontier that we will seek to investigate is the power of our mind.

There is a whole other universe that we can look at in terms of the metaphysical aspects of the power of your mind.

I'm going to keep you grounded and focused however so that you remain aware of the practical everyday changes you can make to your life before you attempt to use telepathy to achieve your goals or to read people's minds!

I want you to become obsessed with happiness and obsessed with enjoying a happy life.

I want you to become addicted to happiness and addicted to feeling good about yourself.

I want you to worship yourself with even 10% of the adoration you give to your "heroes".

Your thoughts directly create your reality. Every single aspect of your life is directly influenced by your thoughts.

Every single aspect.

- Your physical health

- Your mental and emotional health

- Your relationships

- Your ability to attract wealth

- Your ability to socialize

Everything, **absolutely everything** is directly influenced by your thoughts.

Every thought creates a bio-chemical reaction in your body in the form of the production of hormones and other chemicals.

It's a simple process.

Negative thoughts create toxic and destructive chemicals and hormones.

Pleasant thoughts create positive and beneficial chemicals and hormones.

This is a scientific fact.

So, we are going to teach you how to become masters of your thoughts and when you become masters of your thoughts, every area of your life can be vastly improved in exactly the way you choose it to be.

Every successful person in the world today has become successful because they mastered the power of their thoughts. Anybody who first tries to master his world without first mastering himself is on a hiding to nothing.

As mentioned before, a man named *Victor Frankl* survived the holocaust in World War II because he knew that whatever else was happening around him, he had the responsibility for and dominion over his thoughts.

Only he had the power to choose what thoughts he kept in his mind. And that got him through years of hell in the concentration camp.

He made a "Heaven of Hell". Sure, he had a million reasons to be angry and to have hateful thoughts, that would have been easier for him and made more sense. However, he had the knowledge, wisdom and presence to know that hatred begets hatred and that by holding negative thoughts in his own mind, he was only damaging himself during his incarceration.

He chose to give himself emotional and mental freedom by looking at things in a different way, and by choosing to cultivate more useful and beneficial thoughts and feelings.

Do not think for a moment that I am encouraging a la-de-da denial of seeing the world for what it is, and protecting yourself when you can. Yes, you must accept what is but you must also then decide that if you cannot take a particular action to change the external reality, you must then choose what thoughts to hold in your mind for your own health and sanity.

How you look at things, and how to view your world, directly impacts you. Again, you are the ruler of your mind and you must choose whether to make it Heaven or Hell.

How you use your mind to view your world, and how you choose to create beliefs and take actions based on your view of the world, in your mind, is how your life plays out.

There are some schools of thought that dispute the existence of any real objective reality because every single one of us holds our own view of the world.

In other words, who's to say what is real or not?

What's more important for you is how you believe your world to be.

Beliefs are incredibly powerful and much like your daily habits, the beliefs you hold and have held for a lifetime shape your view of the world and shape your reaction to the world.

Many of the beliefs and views you hold about the world have been with you since childhood.

Many of these beliefs were passed down by your parents, which were passed down from their parents, and from their parents.

As I pointed out in an early chapter however, at what point do you say "stop" and ask yourself which of these beliefs do you want to now cast off and what new beliefs do you want to cultivate for yourself?

How do you view yourself?

What do you believe about yourself and about your life?

What limitations do you believe exist for your life?

What do you believe you are capable of?

The answers to these questions exist first and foremost in your mind, long before they will ever manifest in the "real world".

Depending on the answers to these questions, you may choose a range of actions or you may choose no actions, whereby your mental limitations are restricting any action in the real world.

Your mind holds the key to everything in your life.

What the mind can conceive, the mind can achieve.

Whether you believe you can or cannot do something, you are generally correct.

You must now take responsibility for your mind, your thoughts and your actions.

You must and you can choose how to view the world. It's not delusion, it's not denial.

It's about thinking in terms of "what are the possibilities here?", "what can I do?", "what way can I look at this situation so that I am more resourceful to take the correct action?"

It's about no longer reacting to your environment in the same way that our caveman ancestor did. We have developed a reasoning capacity that gives us the ability to choose how to think and how to feel.

We are, in this day and age, now realising the incredible power our mind has in the form of our subconscious mind.

Your Subconscious Mind

What if I told you that every single thing that ever happened in your life was stored in a vast, perhaps limitless (within the confines of normal human life) database, library, store-room or whatever metaphor suits you best?

What if I told you that this same storehouse can handle 2 billion pieces of information at any one time?

And while doing this, it also maintained and managed your heartbeat, your hair growth, your breathing, your cell re-generation, your immune system, and much more, even when you slept.

Imagine if this part of your mind never slept.

Imagine if this part of your mind was like an infinitely powerful and obedient servant that took whatever commands you gave it and did everything in its power to turn that command into reality.

Well, imagine no more, because your subconscious mind does all of this and much more.

Another powerful part of your subconscious mind is that it stores all of your habits and beliefs which are taken away from your every day conscious activity and stored and activated on an unconscious level.

The challenging part about this is that if there are habits and beliefs that no longer serve you, you need to communicate with your subconscious mind in order to re-evaluate these beliefs and change these habits so that they work in your favour as befits somebody of your age and place in life.

The positive part however is that you can work with your subconscious mind using techniques such as visualisation and hypnotherapy in order to rapidly learn new habits, new beliefs and at the same time remove old redundant habits and beliefs.

By working with your subconscious mind, you can harness the limitless power of your subconscious mind in creating new habits, setting new goals, improving your immune system and much more.

Specifically for our purposes here, however, there is something very important you need to learn.

Your subconscious mind believes whatever you tell it, so be very careful what you tell it!

If you go around every day thinking casual thoughts such as "I'm useless, I can't do anything, life is hard" etc, your subconscious mind accepts these thoughts are fact and creates subconscious beliefs to support these "opinions".

What's more, your subconscious actively seeks out evidence, constantly, to support these beliefs.

So, if you believe that "All men are b****rds!", your subconscious mind will do everything it can to find evidence of that. How will it do this?

Well as an example, it will seek out romantic partners for you that fit the bill of "All men are b****rds" and hence continue to generate self-fulfilling prophecies.

The interesting thing about your subconscious mind is that it has no idea of right and wrong, it just faithfully carries out the orders presented to it.

As a result, and once you catch yourself constantly feeding yourself negative thoughts, you can CHOOSE to change the thoughts you feed you mind.

And that's how you need to look at it.

You are feeding your mind thoughts on a constant basis, so you must choose to feed your mind with positive beneficial thoughts of how you want things to be, not how you DO NOT want them to be.

The lesson here is a simple on.

Use your mind to focus on what you DO WANT in life and in any given situation and not on what you don't want.

I could continue with a full lecture series here, but we don't have the time at this point.

The important thing for you to know is that your mind is like a powerful laser and when focused correctly on your positive goals for how you want to be in life, what you want to do in life, and what you want to have in life, it will obey you and will assist you.

Your learning point from this chapter is the following:

- Decide on what you do want

- Use your mind to focus on what you do want

- Feed your mind with positive inspiring thoughts and it will deliver ten fold.

- Your mind is immensely powerful, so work with it.

In a later chapter, we'll look at specific techniques for actually using the power of your mind to achieve real and tangible results for you.

Why we do what we do

Everything happens for a reason they say. When it comes to human behaviour it is absolutely 100% true.

Humans have a wide range of needs to meet, and it is in the nature of our minds and our species to always be seeking to meet a need. In other words, everything we do is an attempt to meet one of our needs.

Another colloquial term puts it nicely as *"if it's not one thing, it's another"*.

Your priorities are your needs. From day to day you have things you need to do, priorities to attend to.

Your mind focuses on what you need most from moment to moment and this is how you prioritise on a deep level or a conscious level what to act on and where to allocate your time and energy.

Very often, at an unconscious level, we have needs we have perhaps not fulfilled and for that reason, we can often find ourselves indulging in habits and behaviours that at other times would seem insane.

The good news for us is that most of the attempts to meet our needs take place on an unconscious level.

The bad news for us is that most of the attempts to meet our needs take place on an unconscious level.

Our good and bad habits are attempts to meet our needs.

Our greatest efforts in life are attempts to meet our needs.

Our most wacky neuroses are attempts to meet our needs.

One of the consequences of this is that, within your unconscious mind, there is no right or wrong, good or bad.

Every behaviour, at this level, is an attempt to meet a need and to go one step further. Every behaviour, has, at some subjective level, a positive intent for the person in question.

When you smoke, you do so to meet a need in a certain situation.

When you drink, you do so to meet a need in a certain situation.

When you lash out at someone in anger, you do so to meet a need in a certain situation.

Context is very important in relation to which need pops up.

Take smoking for example again. When you are playing football, or absorbed in some activity which you love, smoking could be the furthest thing from your mind.

However, drop you in amongst your mates who are smoking and all of a sudden, the context is different, your state of mind is different, and your most immediate need is different and all of a sudden, smoking is not only acceptable but essential in that isolated situation.

Funny huh?

More often than not, these are unconscious and one of the biggest steps you can now make in life, here, is to become aware of where your habits, behaviours and choices are being used, perhaps ineffectively, to meet a need in these isolated situations.

You can become aware of how, although your habit is meeting a need, the price you are paying for that may be way too high.

The good news is that, as always, you can make a small quantum leap in your evolution now and choose to meet your need in a different way.

You can choose a new behaviour or habit to meet your needs and free yourself from the old, out-dated, destructive and redundant behaviours of the past.

As a quick and free tip to weight loss by the way, research has shown that one of the easiest ways to change your eating habits is to keep a daily food diary.

The reason for this?

Very simply, it takes your unconscious eating habits and makes it conscious and puts it on paper in front of you. Awareness is the key.

Our six basic needs

So after all the introductions, red carpet treatment and the pre-conditioning, it's time to formally introduce you to your needs.

Our basic human needs are as follows:

- Your need for *security* or *certainty*

- Your need for *variety* or *uncertainty*

- Your need for *love* or *connection* to others

- Your need for *significance* or recognition

- Your need for *progress* or growth

- Your need for *contribution* or to be of service.

And that's it. If you feel you have other needs, they are in fact manifestations and varieties of these needs and the simpler you can keep it, the better.

Everything you do is an attempt at some level to meet these needs.

In today's society of "achievement" and "performance" it has become somewhat taboo to even admit to having needs and having "needs" is often seen as a sign of weakness or a neurosis!

"She's a nice girl and all but she has needs…"

"Jesus, that guy is so needy, he gets on my nerves."

Everyone has needs. It's only the manner in which you are meeting them that can be neurotic, limiting or damaging.

And trust me, refusing to even accept or acknowledge that you have needs is infinitely more neurotic than being "Needy"!

So step one, you can accept as fact, and be comfortable with it, that you have needs and that you share those needs with everyone.

Having accepted that much already places you in a position of personal power regarding how you choose to meet those needs.

Even taking this step has shot you up the ladder of personal growth and you are already making it possible to wave goodbye to the old habits, behaviours and limitations of the past.

Why You Have That Habit

If your habit, neurosis, behaviour or condition was not meeting a need, it would not exist.

I could probably repeat that a few times such is the importance of it. To save me the bother, I'm going to allow your subconscious mind to let it echo around a few times and see what part of your personality and deeper mind it feels most relevant to.

If you had a more beneficial, enjoyable and productive alternative way to meet whatever need is being met, you would have no need for that limiting habit, condition or behaviour.

Whatever your behaviour or habit it.

Maybe it's smoking, drinking, drugs, bullying, a fear or phobia.

They're all meeting a need and they're all creating conflict and doing you damage.

Your poor subconscious mind is caught between a rock and a hard place.

It "needs" to satisfy your needs, yet it also knows that your behaviours aren't ideal and that's why you "feel" the conflict, unease and ill health.

So, you can now do yourself a favour and continue to learn why you do what you do and how to choose alternative ways to get what you really want and free yourself.

Accept your neuroses as your current best attempt to meet those needs

Reading the Signs

We all share the same basic human needs which drive our behaviours and feelings.

The person who is most aware of their needs and is aware of their behaviour is a person who is primed for a pretty fulfilled life.

It's all about fluidity, flexibility, awareness, movement, dynamism and certainty.

Say for example, you were extremely thirsty and in dire need of hydration i.e. water.

If you lacked the basic awareness to read that signal of thirst, you might try to satisfy that thirst by eating a cheeseburger.

Do you think that would help?

I didn't think so. So it's important to learn the signals from your mind and body so that you can address those needs.

It's like a baby crying. Because a new born baby cannot yet speak English (or whatever language the parents speak), they are not capable of verbalising their needs.

However, the well trained ear can learn to distinguish between the cry that means "hey, I'm starving over here!" and the one that means "I'm tired and need to be hugged and then put to bed" or the one that means "Hmm, I think we need changing here please…"

So, what do you think would happen if the baby uses the "feed me" cry and the parent changes its nappy or if the baby used the "change me" cry and the parents fed him/her?

In fact this is a common error by unsuspecting parents.

A baby cries, it must mean they are hungry.

Every time the baby cries, they get fed.

Regardless what the need is, they get fed.

Fast forward 30 years, not-so-tiny Tim is feeling a little low after a bad day in the office.

What does he do, to relieve the stress? Why, he feeds himself of course!

So, you can get the picture as to how it's important to learn to read the signs, learn the signals.

If you feed the wrong need in the wrong way, you at the very least, do not feed the need at all, and at worst, cause long term damage to yourself.

You can think of it like the dashboard in your car. If the fuel light comes on, what do you do?

You put in petrol or diesel of course. You don't try to further inflate the already inflated tyre. For one thing, the tyre would explode and secondly you haven't correctly recognised the need for fuel, so the car cuts out on a lonely highway.

Not learning to read the signs and heed the signals your mind sends you about your needs results in you using an ineffective behaviour to NOT meet your need and your needs still not being met, so you now have at least two problems.

Your subconscious mind guides you with feelings, moods, hunches, gut instincts, even pains and aches and phobias, as a means of communicating with you to tell you if something is right or wrong.

By having an awareness of yourself, your life, your situation and your feelings, you can use this as a compass to decide whether something in your life needs change or adjustment.

Learn to distinguish between the signals your mind and body send you

How to meet your needs

So how do you fix this then?

When you find yourself indulging in a behaviour or habit that you know at a deep level is in-effective and not for your highest good, ask yourself honestly, "ok which of my needs am I using this behaviour for?"

Are you smoking for confidence? Confidence is certainty. If you are smoking for confidence, think of 3 new ways in which you can feel confident amongst those same people.

Why 3?

Well, 1 option is not an option. 2 options is a dilemma, but 3 options gives your unconscious mind real choice so that smoking is no longer the default "way" you meet your needs.

Are you an addictive texter or do you spend hours online at night? Ask yourself "what is the need here?" Is it a need for connection to other people? Again, come up with 3 new easy ways for you to meet people and connect with people.

Do you have a boyfriend or girlfriend who you have been cheating on? What's the need being met? Are you looking for variety in your life? This is a funny one, because when it comes to relationships, people often get stuck between the needs of certainty and variety.

They want to hang on to the partner they have, even if the love is gone and if they know there is no future.

Yet, it still gives them certainty.

They then choose to have an affair because that gives them variety.

So what do you do?

Well, the choice is yours ultimately BUT, what are the other ways you can bring variety into your relationship so that there is no need to go outside for that variety?

Alternatively, how can you increase the certainty in your own life so that you do not need to cling on to an old relationship and use the other person as your source of certainty?

Let's take another example. Let's say you often get in fights or arguments and refuse to accept that you could ever be wrong, to the point where you lose most of your friends. What need is being met here?

Is it the need for significance or to be important? If so, again, what are 3 new ways that you can become significant without causing arguments? Can you do more in your local sports club? Can you do volunteer work?

This simple technique works for most of your old habits, although in some case, you may need the help of a professional to truly remove some of the unconscious debris, especially if the habits were created during a difficult past event, but that's a discussion for another day.

For now, your learning point is that everything you do is an attempt to meet a need, one of the six needs.

You have the choice to first become aware of that and secondly to choose a new way to meet that need and turn that into a new habit, a new behaviour, a new you.

Self-Awareness and responsibility are the cornerstones of Emotional Intelligence, something that has been sorely lacking amongst many, for a number of years now.

The next section explains the concept of Emotional Intelligence a little more and how by increasing your own EI, your sense of confidence and personal leadership increases.

Emotional Intelligence and Leadership

You are the new leaders and when I say "you", I mean either you, reading this now, or somebody else like you, your age, who will take up the challenge if you do not.

Will you accept the challenge?

Will you accept the challenge to make you a better person and to make better choices?

Will you accept the challenge to change when you can, for the better and to hold a vision of a future for yourself and a vision of a better country and better world?

Will you accept the challenge to be a more authentic, a more real, a more individual you, who knows when to stand out from the crowd when it is the right thing to do?

Will you accept the challenge to be more self aware and to accept responsibility for your thoughts, feelings and actions?

This is what Emotional Intelligence is, and no Leader can exist without it. Emotional Intelligence (or EQ as it is popularly known) is simply your ability to be self-aware, aware of you personally and aware of your social interactions.

It is the awareness of your emotions and the management of these emotions and the management of your relationship with yourself and with other people.

Emotional Intelligence is regarded as being perhaps more important than IQ.

Emotional Intelligence is about not giving in to tantrums and tempers but instead to make decisions from a wiser more mature viewpoint. Emotional Intelligence is about your next step in evolution where you no longer re-act like a caveman, but where you use your intelligent reasoning capacity so you can skilfully blend your emotions and feelings with your keen intellect and make wise choices and focus your mind and energies.

Saints and Scholars is about Emotional Intelligence.

If I was to make it an even simpler description, being Emotionally Intelligent is about acknowledging that you have emotions to begin with and about accepting your emotions, recognising them and working with them.

In generations gone by, to even recognise emotion within yourself was almost regarded as a weakness.

Being courageous with your emotions, capable of sharing them with others, being able to even talk about them is, thankfully, a real sign of leadership today.

In contrast the old "poker up the you-know-what, I feel no emotions" line from Major Dad of yesteryear is a sign of short-sightedness and fear.

As a quick aside, master charismatic leaders such as Presidents Clinton and Obama often littered their speeches with phrases such as "I feel", "I am touched by…" "I yearn for…", all terms of feeling and emotion.

Intellect can go someway to winning respect with people, and building some level of trust, but emotion is true leadership and learning how to tap into your own emotion and share that with others is what leadership and positive influence is all about.

Mastery and the concept of Saints and Scholars are about the unification of your feelings and your intellect. No longer experiencing internal conflict between them but instead reaping the benefits of the synergy of both.

It's akin to the Alchemical Marriage between the beast within and the wisdom from above.

Will you now allow yourself to become aware and to choose differently, choose more wisely for you and to choose to take on worthy challenges for you and for others?

It will take courage to stand out from the crowd initially but that's what real leaders do.

Real leaders don't look for followers. Followers find leaders. Real leaders have authenticity, honesty, purpose, clarity and belief in what they must do and in what they will do even if it is initially an unpopular choice.

Leaders follow these instincts and then they discover that they have followers. To start out to wish for followers is not leadership but a search for popularity. This is not leadership.

You must first be the master and the leader of you. When you have mastered you, are at peace with you and truly know you.

When you have raised your own self-awareness and your awareness of how you relate to and interact with your environment, you are well on the way in this journey.

The new leaders don't need to preach or to make inspiring public speeches. The new leaders lead from within, lead by example and when they have clear motives, a clear mission and a clear mission statement, they have presence and others can recognise that and relate to that.

As mentioned above, leaders lead through emotion because emotion is energy and when you act from a place of Emotional Intelligence you act from a place of internal power.

A very quick description of the basis for Emotional Intelligence, divides into 4 areas which you can easily consider in your own life today.

- Self Awareness

    o How aware are you of your own emotions and feelings?

    o Can you recognise the signals that you are feeling strong emotions?

    o How aware are you regarding your strengths and limitations?

- Self Management

    o Can you manage your emotional urges?

    o Are you comfortable with knowing when and

how to express those emotions or do you just go with every impulse you get?

- o How do you manage yourself in relation to strengths and limitations?

- Social Awareness

    - o Are you aware of the effects of other people on your emotions?

    - o Are you aware of the effects of your emotions on other people?

    - o Are you aware of how you and your emotions are perceived amongst others?

- Relationship Management

    - o How capable are you of dancing the dance between your emotional state and somebody else's, respecting the boundaries and different value sets that may exist?

As you can imagine, all of the technical knowledge in the world only goes so far, but without a positive degree of Emotional Intelligence, and without the ability to manage yourself and your relationships, you either run the risk of "not existing" in one extreme, to being downright obnoxious and avoidable to the other.

So, have a think.

Who do you believe yourself to be?

What feelings and impulses are authentic to you and which are merely fleeting anomalies?

How do you wish to treat others?

How do you wish others to treat you?

You are the Lead Role

There is a saying that goes:

"*The world learns how to treat you by watching how you treat yourself*.

If you feel you deserve respect, then you must show yourself respect.

If you feel you deserve love, then you must show yourself love.

Consider the following from Marianne Williamson:

'Our deepest fear is not that we are inadequate. Our deepest fear is that we are powerful beyond measure. It is our light, not our darkness, that most frightens us.' We ask ourselves, Who am I to be brilliant, gorgeous, talented, fabulous? Actually, who are you not to be? You are a child of God. Your playing small doesn't serve the world. There's nothing enlightened about shrinking so that other people won't feel insecure around you. We are all meant to shine, as children do. We were born to make manifest the glory of God that is within us. It's not just in some of us; it's in everyone. And as we let our own light shine, we subconsciously give other people permission to do the same. As we're liberated from our own fear, our presence automatically liberates others."

How often have you felt that itch of greatness that sometimes dares to swim to the surface and explode in majesty? But then you feel "no I can't, they'll think I'm big headed, too big for my boots, I'll just stay quiet and fit in."

The world is calling upon you and is asking you to make a statement as to how you wish to be treated and how wish to live your life.

You have the power to say no. You have the power to now choose how you wish to be treated and how to treat others.

You are different to your friends, you are different to your siblings and you are different to your parents, although you all have much in common.

You express your differences by saying yes and by saying no. It is your right to an opinion. It is your right to expression.

Do not ever be afraid to say no. You will find that a lot more respect comes your way when you begin to say no at the required times.

The use of yes and no shape your life. The use of yes and no gives your life direction, purpose.

The use of yes and no are your tailfins in life, your steering wheel.

You are at the wheel, and although you may have many back seat drivers, ultimately, if you crash, it's your responsibility.

You are the Lead Role in your life and this is something you must always remember.

If not you, then who?

Your Mission Statement

This is such an important concept that it needs its own chapter. Your Mission statement may change over your life as you change and grow but your Mission statement will always be important and vital to you personally and professionally.

In a later chapter, we'll look at the idea of your Unique Selling Point and what makes you unique.

There are going to be many times in your life when you're going to need your "elevator pitch" which is a jargon term for a quick, clear and concise statement, delivered with certainty, which states who you are, what you stand for and what you do.

You'll need this pitch in job interviews and all manner of social interactions also, but don't think of it as a phoney marketing blurb. This is a real statement of intent.

This is all about your "I Am…" statement and it needs to be honest, clear, authentic and really about you. This is about making a clear statement to the world about who you are and what you hold to be sacred in your life and what lies at the centre of your existence.

So before we go any further, it's time to really nail this. It's time for you, now, with hopefully a greater degree of self awareness, or at least curiosity about yourself, to make a statement about who you are, what you stand for and what you can do.

This is about what you feel your mission in life is.

If you were to sum up in a few words, or sentences, what you instinctively feel that your mission in this life is, what would that be?

Your mission statement should inspire you most of all and be clear to you and leave you in no doubt as to, "yep, that's me".

It should be clear and concise enough so you can show it to your Granny and she can say "yep, that's you."

Your mission statement focuses on and expresses your core values and your core competencies.

Your mission statement can make a bold statement of your intention in life.

This is a vital exercise for everyone to go through and a regular habit needs to be built around such a mission statement, because your mission statement states your mission, it states your purpose, it expresses your motives, your modus operandi and makes it clear to you and the world where your focus lies and where your energies are aimed.

Your Mission Statement tells the world in a few lines just who you are and what you're about.

It's not about a strict formula for writing one. It's about passion and purpose. It's about whatever gets your blood flowing and makes you connect with the undeniable part of you.

My humble advice is to just begin with a pen and paper and start to write about you, write about what you love, what's important to you, write about what you used to be good at, what you are good at and what you would like to be good at. Write about what the perfect day and perfect life would be. Just get it all out on paper, and then sift through it, look for the real highlights. Seek out the details that are undeniably and simply you. Look for the common themes that have occurred at the best times in your life.

When you have completed a brief brainstorm, you can then simply structure your Mission Statement by the following 5 simple steps.

1. Who are you? State who you are, your name, when and where you were born. State your parents' names. This simple opening helps you feel truly unique because you know that there wasn't another one of you born at that moment, in that place, and to those parents.

2. What do you believe and what do you stand for? Write a simple summary of your main values and personal qualities much like your personal constitution. You can state this in the form of "I believe that…" or some variation of this. Again, this is about what you hold to be sacred, this is about "the truths you hold to be self-evident". As outlined on numerous occasions, to not be aware of what you hold to be sacred, or worse, to not hold anything to be sacred you leave yourself open to the mercy of the winds and drift aimlessly with no self-direction.

3. What do you do and what can you do? State your main talents, skills and competencies. This is where you state what you can do and what you want to do. If you find yourself thinking of what you can't do, let the thought slide and get back to what you can do currently and what you would like to expand and grow to be able to do.

4. What is your grand dream of life, your vision? You write what you wish for your life to be on a grand scale, the big picture. This is a brief concise sound bite that projects your vision of the world for all to see and hints towards your larger goals in life. State this as "It is my dream and aim to be..." Don't get caught up on specifics or "how" it might actually happen, just connect with the big vision of who you see yourself being.

5. What will you do on a daily basis? This is about how you commit to living your daily life. All of the best visions and intentions are fairly sterile without disciplined, consistent action on a daily basis. You write your commitments and promises to yourself and to the world of what you will do and how you will live your daily life in making yourself better and making your life continually better.

To make this more effective, write this in the present tense as your subconscious mind operates in the present tense. You can write it as "Every day I..." or "I commit to doing..." for a number of high priority examples of what you want out of life and how you want to continue to improve.

What you have just written is a summary of who you are, what you are about, what you can do, and what you now plan to do to be even better.

If it sounds pretty simple, it's because it actually is. The hard part is getting started of course and the harder part is then to be clear about what you want, and taking the steps to get there.

But for now the important thing is to take the time to create your Mission Statement, because this is the master plan.

From this shall come your individual goals in life and in a later chapter we will look at Goal setting and some of the theories and methods and some of the newer methods which greatly enhance your chances of actually achieving those goals.

Take time **now**, to begin this exercise and make it a habit to remind yourself of who you are, what you stand for, what you can do and what you want to do.

There will come times in your life when certain challenges and difficulties arise, whether that be in relationships or career, and you will doubt yourself. You may believe you have nothing to offer, you may believe you have no worth.

This is when you need to remind yourself of who you are, what you stand for and what you can do and what you choose to do.

Whatever challenge arises in life, remember this.

You existed before the challenge existed. Your abilities, values and the essence of who you are did not, can not and will not disappear over night. You will continue to exist long after that challenge has disappeared.

Taking Action

"Do you want to know who you are?

Don't ask. Act! Action will define and delineate you."

-- Thomas Jefferson

I feel this is a good point to throw in this important concept.

All the good intentions in the world will only go so far, and though I cannot stress enough the importance of being crystal clear about who you are on the inside, because your outer world reflects your inner world, taking action at the right time is essential in creating your life.

Action creates results, results create experience and experience re-enforces your beliefs and self-concept.

So be sure to always take well-intentioned, even small, regular actions so as to move yourself along your path.

Even if the road ahead seems threatening, take a tiny step, dip your toe in the water.

Actions create results. It's also called the GOYA principle i.e. Get Off Your Ass!

This marks the end of this particular section which basically stirred up the waters for you and got you thinking a little more about who you are, what you are capable of, what's important to you and to begin thinking about some areas in your life where you might want to stretch a little, or improve a little

These changes must be chosen by you and for you, because it is your life.

The next chapter goes into detail about how to actually create and achieve the goals you set in life.

They are proven techniques that, if followed as shown, will bring you real changes.

Let's Create the New You

The next part of this book is about actually getting down to creating the new you and setting goals according to your wishes, according to your values and your Mission Statement.

Creating your life from your vision

"I have learned that if one advances confidently in the direction of his dreams, and endeavors to live the life he has imagined, he will meet with a success unexpected in common hours."

- Henry David Thoreau

In previous chapters, you learned a lot about who you are, what you stand for, why you do what you do, and the importance for you to now stand up and be counted as you.

You learned that you and your peers will be the leaders of the future and you must choose now, to become more, do more and then have more.

You have come to the point where you know that the greatest project you will ever undertake in your life is the creation of you as you can be and the creation of your life as it can be.

No matter what you undertake in life, the life-long project of making you better, making you a Saint and a Scholar will be the most important thing you will ever do and will be the greatest commitment you can make in life.

When I say "a better you", I do not mean that there is anything wrong with you currently.

I simply mean that as you grow and change in your life, you will do so in a positive way and with a positive trajectory.

It will be the greatest gift you can give to yourself, your friends and family, your community and your country.

The following sections now help you to take those baby steps and those grand steps to walk towards that future where you are who you were born to be and you do what you were born to do.

Even if you wanted to turn back now, you can't because evolution has already kicked in, my friend.

Even if you decided that it's all too much work, there would be a constant itch annoying you from here on in, dragging you back here.

Welcome to the first steps of becoming the new you.

Your Self Image

Something that is crucial to you achieving any success in any goal and something that underpins many of your expectations of you and of life is your self image.

Your self image is how you see yourself in your mind. Your self image is the opinion you hold of yourself and your beliefs about what you are and are not capable of.

Related to your self image or self concept is your idea of your ideal self or who you would wish yourself to be. Note that this is how you would wish yourself to Be and not Have. Again, we are brought back to the important point that most of your self-development work is in helping you to "Be" a better person and from there you can Do more and then Have more.

The gap that exists between how you currently see yourself and how you wish to be is a powerful influence on your life.

If the gap between these two concepts is relatively narrow and your self concept is pretty close to your ideal self, then you can expect to have a fair degree of contentment and certainty in your life.

Of course beware, as perhaps your "ideal self" is in no way challenging to you and therefore you are simply in a comfort zone?

If on the other hand, the gap between your self image and your ideal self is a wide gaping wound, then this can have two effects.

One, it can make you feel incredibly motivated to change and improve and achieve more of the resources and qualities of your ideal self, or two, it can leave you feeling deflated and lamenting your dominant poor self-image.

The important point for us here, though, is for you to become honestly aware of your current self image.

Honesty is crucial because if you cannot have honesty with yourself, you cannot have a clear awareness of where you are on your journey, and if you do not have an honest awareness of where you currently are, you will find it very difficult to make real and measurable progress to wherever it is you want to go and be.

Your self image is tied in with your values, philosophies and Mission statement which we encountered previously.

Take some time to remind yourself of what you became aware of during those chapters and exercises.

In particular, recall your Mission Statement. When you identified your beliefs, expectations and strengths, did you feel inspired in any way? Did you feel satisfied that this was really you and this was a "you" that you were happy to be day by day?

If not, what were the improvements you identified for yourself, what were the areas of development that you noted that you felt would bring you closer to the you that you deserve to be?

This is an important point because as we progress to actually setting some of your goals, the goals will have conditions. The goals need to belong to you and be personal to you.

The goals need to have motivation and desire behind them and the goals needs to have a degree of challenge to them so that even if the end result is not exactly what you set out to achieve, the actual journey towards it brings its own benefits and you grow as a person.

And that journey is almost as important if not more important than the goal itself.

Before we progress, give yourself permission now to grow. Give yourself permission to see yourself in a better light.

Give yourself permission to believe that you can be more than you were yesterday and that the only real limits that exist for you are, and always were, in your mind and that whatever limitations you may encounter in the outside world, it is the inner obstacles that will always stop you first.

Choose to believe that life can be better and you can be better.

Choose to have an image of yourself in your mind which is resourceful, skilful and capable and which can overcome any of the challenges you previously faced in life.

Believe there are more things in life that you can do that you cannot.

Believe that you control the limitations in your life and that you can choose how to prepare and how to improve in order to exceed those limitations and set higher expectations.

Life rarely turns out as you "wanted" but almost often turns out as you expected. Set your own expectations now and don't simply continue with the ones you were programmed with since birth.

Choose your own self-image now and not simply keep the one that you learned through family and social circles and peers.

Inner reflection is needed in order for you to choose your self image and set your expectations and goals for your life.

It is your life, so make them your goals. They in no way have to have anything in common with your family's goals or your peers' goals. They are your goals for your life.

This is the time when you change how you do things and this is the time when you specify what those changes are to be to make your life better and to make you better.

That is what setting goals is about. Making you better.

To a woman who complained about her destiny the Master said, "It is you who make your destiny."

"But surely I am not responsible for being born a woman?"

"Being born a woman isn't destiny. That is fate. Destiny is how you accept your womanhood and what you make of it."

Creating Your Future – The Power of Focused Intention

At this point, you've come to a deeper awareness of who you are and what you're about. You've outlined your values and principles and perhaps even drafted your constitution in life.

You have also become aware of your boundaries in life and you have remembered and understood, times, situations and people in your life where you previously failed to assert your boundaries or respect the boundaries of others.

And then you learned how to change that and you learned that saying yes and no is the manner in which you direct your life, your thoughts, your actions and these choices and decisions are in fact the tailfins of your craft as you navigate through life.

Having undergone this growth and to a great extent, a cleansing on many levels, this chapter now provides you with the opportunity to now choose what you would wish to have in your life.

There are only minor rules in specifying your plans, desires and intentions.

Before you began reading this book, you may have had vague dreams, visions, plans and wishes and they may have been tinted or even tainted by your life experiences, good and bad, up to that point.

Now, you can start anew if you like, and create goals and plans purely from who you are and what you are destined for.

Now, from your new level of awareness of who you are, you can, using proven techniques, actually begin to achieve those goals. So much so, that if you follow these steps, you can become part of the 3% of mankind that succeeds in the journey they set out on. More on this 3% later…

Are you up to it?

What you need for this success are Clarity, Focused intention, Desire and Discipline to execute the work needed. But it's not even work because it's all for you. You make the rules.

Vision, Clarity and Focus

As you begin to think about how you want your life to pan out, and what you want your life to be, there are a number of very important variables for you to consider.

First, and this is a huge element of being a leader for yourself and for others, is a vision. This is similar to your Mission Statement.

What is your Vision for you and your life? What is that big picture that really represents you and inspires you?

Your vision is your main target, and when you encounter various challenges and yes, setbacks, it is your vision that gives these challenges perspective.

Second, clarity is essential. Clarity is the quality of your vision and moves it from being a vague "sort of a wish" to being a measurable and real target where you can focus. Clarity brings your vision into focus so you can measure your progress.

Clarity helps you to define why you want your goal and your vision.

Clarity helps you to define the real underlying reasons for you wanting your goal.

Clarity keeps you in touch with yourself and your instincts as you work towards your goal.

Third, is focus. Focus makes everything else that is not a priority or not important fade into the background. Focus helps you to place all of your energy on your immediate task, so much so, that there is no room for doubt, hesitation and equivocation.

Without focus, you simply forget what you were meant to do, and why, and you just drift. Focus is like a tractor beam which draws you towards your goal. When you are focused, time loses all meaning. When you are focused, you are in the zone.

Focus is a skill. Some people can do it more naturally than others but everyone can practice it and improve at it.

Focus is most definitely a skill lacking in today's society and most definitely one of the single greatest skills you can teach yourself or learn from others.

There are many ways to practice focus, including Yoga, Tai Chi, Hypnosis and Meditation. All of these disciplines and arts help you to focus your mind completely in the present and to block out all unnecessary distractions.

The benefits are immense, but instead of me giving you a lecture now, just do a Web search on these art forms and you'll find a plethora of articles on the benefits and techniques involved.

When you understand these three ingredients, the disciplined execution of action becomes almost automatic and that's when the results begin to happen quickly and with the expectation of success that you have created for yourself.

Let's continue…

The Harvard Experiment

In the 1950's a now famous experiment was carried out in Harvard University in the US.

It was found that out of a particular class; only 3% had written specific goals for themselves.

In a follow up study some 30 years later, it was found, that although all of the individuals came from similar backgrounds in terms of wealth and opportunity, the 3% who had written goals for themselves had significantly happier, wealthier, more satisfied and content lives than the other 97%.

Make no mistake. The power of having goals, clarifying them, specifying them, and writing them down is vital and essential to ensuring the direction of your life and the success of your life, on your terms.

If you don't choose goals and direction for your life, others will do it for you.

Is that really what you want?

All those times when you wish people would just leave you alone and let you do what you want to do. Well ok, then, what do you want to do?

What do you want?

That is often the hardest question to answer.

Today, you are going to learn about how important written goals are.

You are going to learn how to specify those goals clearly and you are going to learn about how to incorporate those goals into your life.

You are going to learn proven techniques for specifying those goals to maximise the possibility of them actually becoming true.

Having written goals gives you the power to direct your life. Having your goals written down effectively creates a point of focus for your energies and actions.

When you have a clear goal, about which you are passionate, you can never be bored because you enjoy the steps you take on the way to your goal.

Medical research has even shown that people who have clear goals and "something to live for" can actually live longer. A tip for a long life then is to set yourself an attractive goal for how to celebrate your 100th birthday in a fantastic way! Anyone for Vegas?

Having these grand goals provides a place of certainty for you, and provides a backdrop to your life so that all of life's challenges are viewed against your goals and very often you realise that many of life's challenges can be ignored as a result.

Having your goals provides a much higher probability of you achieving the life you often dream of.

Dreams are great, keep dreaming. Now is the next important step, write that dream down.

The greatest architects in the world need to actually sketch out their designs.

Ferrari's chief engineers have to sit down and draw the car they wish to build.

Steven Spielberg still needs to write his 1,000 page movie.

Take your dreams and visions from your imagination and commit them to paper and that is the first very real step to making it a physical reality.

It is more than simply an exercise in discipline or homework.

Once you commit your goal to paper, things begin to happen. Larger forces begin to move and your subconscious mind becomes focused and we all know by now what wonderful things can happen when we focus the power of our subconscious mind.

Playing to your Strengths

My mother said to me, "If you become a soldier, you'll be a general; if you become a monk, you'll end up as the Pope." Instead, I became a painter and wound up as Picasso.

- Pablo Picasso

In a bit, you're going to learn the actual mechanics and techniques for goal setting and what good, effective goal setting involves.

You are in fact going to learn how to use the same goal setting techniques as used by Olympic athletes, business legends, as well as all leaders in every field of life.

So, the only question you may have is:

"What goal will I choose or what sort of goals do I need to be setting for my life?"

The obvious sort of ideas that will jump into your mind will involve phrases such as Ferraris, money, super models, yachts etc etc.

Not so fast. There are certain rules to goal setting.

There are also some philosophies that are worth considering when you think about what goals to choose for your life, and in effect what steps you now want to take in your life.

The first philosophy is the title of this section, which is about playing to your strengths.

If you ask Michael Jordan what sort of goals he used to set for himself, I doubt they were about sculpture or painting.

If you ask Padraig Harrington about his goals, they probably don't include winning a Nobel Prize for physics.

Now, they might, but I'm betting they don't.

One of the ironies of the education system is that if you are struggling in a particular subject, you put more work into that subject instead of actually focusing on what you are good at and achieving a level of Mastery and becoming an expert in something you are good at and actually enjoy.

Yes, we all need a certain proficiency in the basic modules of education, but is it not equally important that we find out early in play, early in your life, where your strengths, talents and passions lie?

All of the most successful people in the world are successful in something they are good at and are passionate about.

So, a major stepping stone we're going to take here is:

Play to your strengths!

Remember our journey so far in this book.

It's about becoming self-aware, knowing yourself, understanding yourself more as a means to then apply both your intellect and your unique philosophies into making your life better.

If that is the case, then does it not make sense to choose goals that focus on your strengths, your true self and your passions?

Of course is does.

So, let's look at some other ideas and concepts around where your strengths lie.

The Areas of Intelligence

> *"It wasn't so much that there were gaps in his knowledge but more that there were islands in his ignorance!"*
>
> *Winston Churchill*

Let's take a few moments to cover an area that is rarely examined.

We all assume that "Intelligence" is purely down to people's IQ or their general academic ability in school.

If somebody is taking all honours in their Leaving Cert, they're assumed to be "intelligent". If somebody is taking no honours in their Leaving Cert, they're assumed to be not so intelligent.

This is not so.

This is what was traditionally known as "book smart". But as research has uncovered, book smart is not the only type of smart that exists and is not even necessarily the most important type of "smart".

Everybody is good at something, even if not covered by traditional educational models or curricula.

I would have been considered one of the intelligent ones in my school and I went on to accumulate a range of degrees and diplomas as I'm an academic sort of a chap. I hold a degree in Electronic Engineering from the best Engineering course in the country (and arguably Europe) in Dublin City University.

However, if I want to install a stereo in my car, I call a friend of mine, who is a Prison Officer??

If I wanted to change the oil in my car, I'd call another guy who didn't even sit the Leaving Cert Exam?

I know how important my car is to me for transport and I know how much I like to have the stereo on while I drive, so I know how vitally important it is to my quality of life that these services have been provided, but it's not important that I know how to do it!

Thankfully, there has been a lot of research in recent years into areas of Intelligence which were previously either ignored or disregarded because they were not part of the reductionist, academic model.

The following are a list of areas of intelligence which are now recognised today and to satisfy the scientists who demand "evidence" for everything, each area of intelligence has also been linked to specific brain functions with their own home in the brain.

So, just as numerical and linguistic intelligence are real signs of intelligence, so are the other areas.

Take a look at the list below and see which of these areas you feel that you are particularly strong in.

You may even like to score yourself on a scale of 1-10 and build up a picture of your overall map of intelligence.

- **Literacy Intelligence**: How comfortable are you with words, reading and writing? How good is Tiger Woods at these things? I don't know and I don't care.

- **Numerical Intelligence**: How comfortable are you with calculations, logical and systematic thinking? How good was Shakespeare?

- **Spatial Intelligence**: Can you "see the whole picture", visualise and outcome? Without visionaries, who would invent anything?

- **Physical (sports, dance etc) Intelligence**: Are you well co-ordinated, capable at physical activities? Was Pele good at Maths?

- **Musical**: Do you have an appreciation of music and its effects on human emotions? Was Beethoven any good at long division?

- **Natural Intelligence**: Do you have an awareness of humans and their interconnectedness with their environment? I wonder how much Jacque Cousteau or David Attenborough enjoyed their Accounting and Finance classes?

- **Interpersonal Intelligence**: Do you get on well with others and display natural empathy? If you don't get on well with people, it doesn't really matter how clever you are. Who'll listen to you??

- **Intrapersonal Intelligence**: How well do you understand yourself? Enough said really?

- **Spiritual Intelligence**: Do you sense that the physical/concrete world that you witness daily is not all there is? Do you sense that there are other things unseen that we cannot see or touch and are a mystery but which still influence our lives? Is anyone going to suggest that the great classical Philosophers were not intelligent?

- **Emotional Intelligence:** Emotional Intelligence is now recognised as being more powerful than traditional Intelligence, simply because when we make decisions, it is our Emotions which often make them for us. Even in big business and big politics where a rational mind is valued above all else, it is Emotional Intelligence or lack thereof, which rules the day and you only have to witness the global events of the past few years to find proof of that.

Certainly, we should have "some" ability in all of these areas, simply because we are capable, but do not define yourself as being Intelligent or not Intelligent based on one of these classifications only.

How much joy have all of our sports stars, musicians and actors brought to our lives despite not being mathematical geniuses?

Richard Branson left school at 14, and focused his passions on what he was good at. As a note of caution, don't think "school is useless" just because Richard Branson left at

14. He had visions and plans that we worked tirelessly towards to achieve.

Henry Ford famously stated that there was no use in him learning loads of information when he could pick up the phone and call one of his employees who knew what he wanted to know.

Einstein similarly stated that he saw no value in trying to memorise information that he could easily find in a book.

Intelligence is not knowledge. Intelligence is the application of knowledge.

So before we start setting goals to bring us success and riches, let's be sure that these are built upon knowledge of who we are and what we enjoy, and using our core competencies.

Your Path of Mastery

In addition to what area of Intelligence you may be strongest in, there are also your natural strengths, talents and passions in life.

This is by no means a fixed formula for how to choose your goals in life, but when you combine these clues together, it may give you a clearer picture of the direction you wish your life to go, where your strengths lie and the sort of goals you can set for yourself to move along that road.

So, if you're ready, just read over the following questions and pay attention to the first answers that come into your mind. It is very often the first answer that comes to mind which is most true for you.

Step 1

Very simply, what do you like to do? Forget about what you feel you are or are not good at. What do you simply like to do? We need to become aware of what we enjoy first before we let our conditioned "can't" voice interrupt!

I Love to…..?

Step 2

What qualities best describe you currently? It's important to be honest here and choose what "is". The next section allows you to choose what you would like to be, so for now, it is essential to clearly and honestly state what the reality is.

I Am……?

Step 3

Now you can state what qualities you would like to have as a person and what you would like to be able to express in your life. What would you like to have more of (qualities, not possessions) and what would you like to be more of? Very often, when it comes to setting Goals, these are good places to start.

I Would Like to Have More/Be More….?

Step 4

In what sort of situations do you stand out and shine?

I shine when (what situations?)

I excel at (what tasks?)

Step 5

It's important to know when you feel like yourself, and feel authentic.

I am most myself when….?

What I do effortlessly is

Step 6

Very often, we find ourselves being drawn to the same sorts of books, music and situations.

I keep being drawn to….?

Step 7

Everyone has an area of expertise, something they've always been the "go to guy/girl" for. :

Think back to when you were younger, hanging out with your friends…

What was your "role" in the group, what were you considered an expert at?

What were you the "go to guy/girl" for?

If there was no such thing as money, and everyone had to use their most natural skill to barter and exchange for goods and services, what tasks or service would you provide?

Step 8

If you were independently wealthy and money was no longer an object, what would you spend your time doing?

Describe your ideal and perfect day including the things you are both good at and love to do.

Now, take a few minutes, to read over everything you have written, absorb it, let it sink in, and let it actually form a picture of who you are at heart. Imagine being the person you have just described, fully.

See it, hear it, and feel it.

Putting it all together then

Now, without analysing too much, feeling as relaxed and natural and possible and if everything in the world was right for you, if you had all the support and resources you needed, taking all of the answers you have provided, what does it appear that your "life business" is? Where do your strengths lie?

If you were to choose a path of Mastery for yourself, what would that path be?

"My path of Mastery is……………?"

I encourage you now, to go for a cup of tea/coffee or marmite and have a think about a goal you would like to set for yourself in relation to an area of your life that you have a passion and a talent for.

Creating your Goals

Ok, at last we've gotten you to the important section about how to actually create and achieve goals for your life.

We're going to use a combination of three techniques:

1. The concept of SMART goals

2. Well Formed Outcomes from the world of NLP.

3. GROW goals from the world of performance coaching.

I have below combined these techniques so you can be sure that you have the very latest and most powerful framework for achieving your goal.

So, before we even attempt to set goals, let's look at the mechanics of these goal setting techniques.

First, I'll introduce the concepts involved and then we'll have a specific template for you to use, so don't get too bogged down in the details just yet!

Correctly Setting your Goals

There are a number of "rules" and methods out there for specifying your goals and I'm going to take a few moments to summarise them here and by all means, feel free to do further research on them for more background information.

These guidelines help you to think about your goals and plans differently so that they become more focused, effective and achievable.

SMART Goals

SMART stands for:

- Specific

- Measurable

- Acceptable

- Realistic

- Time phased

So, let's look at these in a little more detail using your goals that you have come up with.

Specific: A specific goal has a much greater chance of being accomplished than a general goal. To set a specific goal you must answer the six "W" questions:

Who: Who is involved?

What: What do I want to accomplish?

Where: Identify a location.

When: Establish a time frame.

Which: Identify requirements and constraints.

Why: Specific reasons, purpose or benefits of accomplishing the goal.

EXAMPLE: A general goal would be, "Get in shape." But a specific goal would say, "Join a health club and workout 3 days a week for at least 1 hour."

Measurable: Establish concrete criteria for measuring progress toward the attainment of each goal you set. When you measure your progress, you stay on track, reach your target dates, and experience the exhilaration of achievement that spurs you on to continued effort required to reach your goal.

To determine if your goal is measurable, ask questions such as......How much? How many? How will I know when it is accomplished?

Acceptable: To be acceptable, also means to be ecological and to be for your highest good and also for the good of anyone it impacts. A goal cannot simply have a short term gain for you if it has a negative long term pain. This would lead to a conflict of values for you. So this detail requires congruence in terms of the motivations of the goal.

Realistic: To be realistic, a goal must represent an objective toward which you are both *willing* and *able* to work. A goal can be both high and realistic; you are the only one who can decide just how high your goal should be. But be sure that every goal represents substantial progress. A high goal is frequently easier to reach than a low one because a low goal exerts low motivational force. Some of the hardest jobs you ever accomplished actually seem easy simply because they were a labor of love.

Your goal is probably realistic if you truly *believe* that it can be accomplished. Additional ways to know if your goal is realistic is to determine if you have accomplished anything similar in the past or ask yourself what conditions would have to exist to accomplish this goal.

Timed: Timed relates to having a specific deadline towards which you can set specific actions to reach your goal. If you do not have a timed deadline in place, there is no urgency and no motivation to work on it today. You want your goal by December, but what you do today gets you there.

Well Formed Outcomes

Well Formed Outcomes come from the world of Neuro Linguistic Programming (NLP) and it essentially provides a template and a framework for specifying and describing your goals.

It uses a series of questions which shape your goal and discipline you to create a goal that really is under your control, achievable, desirable and specifies the steps you can take to achieve it while also helping you to identify the obstacles you could face.

So it really is an in-depth plan, when, if followed, maximizes your probability of success.

A very important rule for all goals, but especially Well Formed Outcomes is to specify your goal in the POSITIVE i.e. to state what you DO want to happen as opposed to what you DON'T want.

The basic questions which are asked in Well Formed Outcomes are as follows, and we will expand on them in more detail in just a bit:

1. What is your desired goal, stated in the positive?

2. How will you know when you have achieved it?

3. What will achieving this do for you, what will you gain, what are the benefits?

4. What will achieving this help you avoid or avoid feeling?

5. How will others know that you have achieved it, how will you be different?

6. When do you want this goal achieved by?

7. Are there any situations where you do not want this?

8. What additional skills or resources do you need to achieve this?

9. Is this something you yourself can achieve or are there other people you need to help you?

10. What are the benefits of you achieving this?

11. What would you lose by achieving this?

12. Are there any alternatives to this goal for you?

13. What options are open to you now to achieve this goal?

14. What steps can you take towards achieving this goal?

15. What can you do right now?

You will see a little later how important these questions are, and before you throw your eyes up to heaven and say "if I thought it was this much work I wouldn't have bothered!"

Well, guess what. That's exactly why only 3% of the population do this, and why only 3% of the population really succeed.

Real planning and goal setting is a job, and if you can't muster up the discipline and motivation to do this much, then how can you expect to be able to persevere in the face of periodic set-backs and disappointments?

Remember, potential, talent and great ideas count for nothing without the application of effort, preparation, perseverance, determination and discipline.

Have patience, invest your energies with focus and the rewards will come.

GROW Model for Goals

The GROW Model for goal setting comes from the world of performance coaching which is used with top athletes, business executives and basically all high achievers.

In fact to repeat the point, these techniques combined are THE most powerful way for you to set and achieve your goals.

So, what does GROW stand for?

GROW is mnemonic and stands for:

- Goal: What do you want?

- Reality: Where are you currently in

relation to your goal? What obstacles or resources exist?

- Options: What options are open to you to pursue your goal?

- Work: What specific steps need to be taken by whom and when in order to achieve your goal?

Again, I will only give a brief description here, but when we get to our template, each portion will be described in detail.

An important concept in the GROW model is that you have different levels of goals.

1. Your overall goal. This is your end game, your dream goal e.g. to win the cup final. These goals tend to be out of your control in that there are other factors and variable which you cannot control such as the opposition, the referee, the weather, the pitch etc. So the overall goal provides the backdrop and the motivation for your efforts. This is the prize.

2. Your process goal. This is your task, your personal goal. This specifies what needs to be done in order to make your overall or dream goal a reality. In our example, your process goal is to become the best player you can be, the best team you can be, to become fitter, stronger, and more skilful. Again, the important word here is "what". Your process goal is "what" you need to become.

3. Your Work goal. These are the specific baby steps

and these are the goals you must set on a daily basis for yourself. These are the goals over which you have full control and ownership and which you can feel 100% confidence working towards. The pursuit and achievement of these goals makes you better, helps you achieve goal 2 and maximise your chances, but does not guarantee the overall goal. Nevertheless, by simple achieving these goals you gain so much more along the journey that benefit you in far more ways. Again, these are the steps you take on a consistent daily basis and to even get in the healthy habit of applying yourself to the work goals, you benefit enormously. A big question regarding these steps is "what are you prepared to invest in your goal? What are you prepared to do or what are you prepared to sacrifice or give up even in order to achieve your goal?"

So you can now imagine, how combining all of the techniques above in a clear framework, which I will give you, will really shape your goal for you and lay out in clear steps how you get from where you are to where you want to be.

SMART Well Formed Outcomes for helping you to GROW

Yes, yes I know, a completely contrived name but it'll be worth it.

Step 1:

Stated in the positive, what do you want? In your own words, what is your goal?

This is your overall goal, your dream goal, your vision. It could be a tangible object such as building a house, getting a job, or it could be an internal goal, such as a resource you want to develop, such as more confidence, more focus for exam study.

This question is not concerned with "how" your going to get it just yet, this is a simple short title and statement for your goal.

It must be stated in the positive and not as "I don't want…"

e.g. "My goal is to compete in the next national athletics championships"

State your overall goal here:

_____

_____

_____

_____

_____

_____

Step 2:

Is this something you have chosen for yourself and over which you have control? Is this your goal?

If this goal has not been chosen by you, and is not something you are personally invested in, then the likelihood is that at the first hurdle or real obstacle, you will make your excuses and refuse to jump the fence.

The choice must be yours and it must be something you want for yourself.

At the very least, if it is proposed by somebody else, you must buy into it 100% and adopt it as your own.

_____

_____

_____

_____

_____

_____

_____

Step 3:

How will you know when you have achieved it?

Describe the moment of triumph in full descriptive sensory terms and in the present tense. This is a very important step. You need to be able to clearly experience it mentally in every detail if you want to be able to expect it physically. Additionally, when you learn to use your imagination fully and really experience it mentally, you will also feel the emotions associated with achieving your goal. This will give rise to an endorphin and dopamine rush in your mind and body.

As your inner mind can not tell the difference between an imagined and real occurrence, your unconscious mind will believe you have already achieved it, and as such will then believe that you can achieve this.

Between the endorphins, the dopamine and the inner mind's expectation of success, your mind and body become programmed and motivated to pursue your goal.

On the contrary, if your "vision" lacks clarity, focus and feeling, your unconscious mind will find it much harder to motivate you and direct you towards your goal.

So, in full poetry and expression, describe in the present tense your moment of triumph and achievement:

"I see myself....

_____
_____ "

"I can hear....

_____
_____ "

"I feel... _____
_____ "

Again, let loose on this step, write as much as you want in as much clarity.

For the visual elements, describe each object you see, the colours, the brightness. Really bring it to life.

Make the image and associated sensory elements so clear and inspiring that they are unmistakable and make a real impression on you.

Step 4:

What will achieving this really do for you? What will it give you and what will it help you avoid?

What will be the benefits of achieving this?

This question highlights your motivations and if your "why" is strong enough here, you will feel more empowered and capable of overcoming inevitable obstacles that will appear.

If your reason and your motivation is not clear and strong enough, then you may have difficulty persevering.

Very often, our reasons can be positive i.e. "This will give me a great sense of pride in myself"

Equally as often, our reasons can be not so positive but equally powerful i.e. "This will take away my feelings of not being good enough around people." It's one of those cases of using pain to motivate yourself.

This is what is known as being motivated Towards something positive or Away from something negative.

It is usually more beneficial to have a combination of the two, being especially clear about what you are moving towards because that's the way your mind essentially works.

Also, very often, by becoming aware of these motivations, we can identify underlying motivations that may become goals in their own right.

For example, if the benefit was something like above i.e. "feeling more pride", then a sub goal here is for you to actually feel more pride.

As a result, you can then identify more options to achieving more pride even if competing in the Olympics was not an option, so you still get to satisfy the underlying need.

So, what will be the benefits of you achieving your goal?

_____
_____
_____
_____
_____
_____
_____
_____

Step 5:

What will be the consequences of you not achieving this?

This is another leg of the motivation stool. If you don't make the change, if you don't pursue the goal, what will be the price you will pay? How will you suffer?

This is pain motivation you make clear to yourself so as you are motivated to persist and persevere with your goal.

e.g. "If I do not make this change, and pursue a healthy lifestyle, I could put on weight, get fat, become unattractive and put my health at risk."

Don't be afraid to crank up the emotion on this, because it is that emotional leverage that can get you off your ass as they say.

Also, make it real and relevant to you so that it does make you want to make those changes.

_____

_____

_____

_____

_____

_____

_____

_____

_____

Step 6:

How will others know that you have achieved it, how will you be different? What other people does this effect?

Looking from the outside in, how will you look and behave differently, once you have achieved your goal. How will people know? What will you be able to do now, that you couldn't do before?

_____

_____

_____

_____

_____

_____

_____

_____

_____

Step 7:

How close are you to your goal currently?

This question is an awareness raiser for you. This is where you need to be honest with yourself because if you cannot honestly assess where you are now, your attempts to get to your goal will be severely hampered.

For example, if your goal is to lose weight or to achieve a specific weight and size, you need to know exactly what weight and size you are now, so that you can track your progress over time and set periodic goals for yourself.

_____

_____

_____

_____

_____
_____
_____
_____

Step 8:

When do you want this goal achieved by?

This is a very simple but important step. By giving your unconscious mind a realistic and achievable timeframe, it produces just enough urgency without too much stress.

You want to have the perfect balance of challenge v stress for yourself. You will know the honest answer here.

_____
_____
_____
_____
_____
_____
_____
_____

Step 9:

What would you lose by achieving this?

A strange question to ask you might say, but a very important one.

I made the point earlier that every single behaviour we have, has a positive intent at some level. If there was no benefit or positive intent to it, we wouldn't do it, fact.

For this reason, we again, need to become honestly aware of what our old behaviour was giving us and what we could lose by changing to our new goal.

As an example, consider smoking.

Some people smoke for confidence, so to just stop smoking without coming up with alternative strategies for confidence we leave ourselves out on a limb.

So, for this step, be honest and state what you feel you could lose by pursuing a certain goal.

At the very least, by being aware of it, it will not be able to secretly sneak up later and scupper your plans.

_____
_____
_____
_____
_____
_____
_____
_____

Step 10:

Name three other options for achieving this?

This gives you the opportunity to specify 3 other strategies for covering the "loss" of whatever secondary benefit you may have been getting from your old behaviour.

_____

_____

_____

_____

_____

_____

_____

Step 11:

What unique personal qualities, resources or skills do you have which support you in this goal?

For you to have chosen this goal, you must have some feeling that you are "qualified" to achieve it or have many of the necessary resources to achieve it.

Why do you believe this goal is for you?

_____

_____

_____

_____

_____

_____

_____

_____

Step 12:

Is this something you yourself can achieve or are there other people you need to help you?

Is this goal within your own control or do you need to identify other people to help you?

For example, do you need a coach or a mentor to help you in your activities?

_____
_____
_____
_____
_____
_____
_____
_____

Step 13:

What is currently standing in your way externally and internally?

What additional skills or resources do you need to achieve this?

What internal or external obstacles exist between you and your goal?

This is a very important part of any goal or project. You need to sit down and appraise the situation and identify any obstacles within you or externally that may need to be overcome.

For example, do you have an internal fear or limiting belief about your capabilities that needs to be re-framed and overcome in order for you to really believe you can achieve this?

If necessary, do you need new skills or personal qualities in order to achieve your goal?

_____

_____

_____

_____

_____

_____

_____

_____

Step 14:

What are you prepared to invest or sacrifice in pursuing this goal? What makes this goal sacred? What are you prepared to do to achieve it?

This is the measure of your commitment to your goal. For a change to occur, for an improvement to occur, very often something needs to be sacrificed if even temporarily.

For example, if you are pursuing and athletic goal, it could be that your social life becomes altered for a time so as you can get in the correct physical condition.

What is the price you are willing to pay in order to achieve your goal?

How important is it to you really?

_____
_____
_____
_____
_____
_____
_____
_____

Step 15:

What options are open to you now to achieve this goal?

What are some of the potential plans or directions you can take now to achieve your goal?

Now that your goal is qualified and you have identified and mitigated against potential pitfalls, what performance goal do you need to identify for yourself?

e.g. "I need to improve my lap times by 3 seconds every week" or "I need to create a workable gym workout plan."

_____
_____
_____
_____

_____

_____

_____

_____

Step 16:

What specific steps can you take towards achieving this goal?

What are the specific steps you need to take every day towards your goal?

e.g. "I need to run X miles 3 days a week" or "I need to spend 1 hour in the gym, every Monday, Wednesday and Friday." Or "I need to follow workout routine X on day X". Or "I will write 2 pages of my book every night."

These are specific steps you take on a consistent daily basis towards your goal. These are the mechanical actions if you like. You should be 100% clear and confident about these steps and if not, they should be reduced further so that the steps you have chosen are 100% achievable.

_____

_____

_____

_____

_____

_____

_____

_____

Step 17:

What can you do right now?

There is nothing better than having an immediate action you can take immediately so that you can commit yourself to your goal.

It is often even more inspiring if you take an impulsive action that makes it hard for you to back out of your goal.

_____
_____
_____
_____
_____
_____
_____
_____
_____
_____

Burn the Boats

In February 1519, Hernando Cortez set sail on the final leg of an ocean voyage that was to take him from Cuba to the distant shores of the Yucatan.

He commanded 11 ships with more than 500 soldiers, 100 sailors, and 16 horses, bound for Mexico to take the world's greatest treasure. The rare jewels, gold, silver, and sculptures sheltered on the Yucatan had been hoarded by the same army for 600 years. Cortez he had heard of riches of the people. With his men they arrived on shore. They did not go and take the treasure, they waited until they were ready. Then Cortez told his men to burn their boats. The men were outraged wondering how they were going to get back to their families. Cortez told them to burn the boats and they would conquer the Yucatan people and gain their fortune. They would take their boats home.

So often, we give ourselves a back-up plan. We want to make sure that we have something in place if things go wrong. By giving yourself the back-up plan, that becomes the plan.

Again, at this point, to re-assure and remind you further of the reason for this exercise:

The people in the world, who are successful, happy, content and wealthy, use these techniques.

The people in the world, who have built their own businesses, live their dreams, enjoy financial, emotional and creative freedom use these techniques.

Professional athletes use these techniques.

Using these techniques, and aligning yourself to specified goals which are an expression of yourself, provide a form of protection for you when life gets a little rough.

Using these techniques help you withstand the sometimes unpredictable gusts of wind that threaten to knock you off your course.

We will deal with such challenges and obstacles in the next chapter but for now, rest assured that by mastering these techniques, all of these techniques, you are mastering your lives.

Each, even small, alteration you make now will have a positive snowball effect on your life moving forward.

Overcoming Obstacles and Challenges

In ancient times, a King had a boulder placed on a roadway. Then he hid himself and watched to see if anyone would remove the huge rock. Some of the land's wealthiest merchants and courtiers came by and simply walked around it. Many loudly blamed the king for not keeping the roads clear, but none did anything about getting the stone out of the way. Then a peasant came along carrying a load of vegetables. Upon approaching the boulder, the peasant laid down his burden and tried to move the stone to the side of the road. After much pushing and straining, he finally succeeded. After the peasant picked up his load of vegetables, he noticed a purse lying in the road where the boulder had been. The purse contained many gold coins and a note from the king indicating that the gold was for the person who removed the boulder from the roadway. The peasant learned what many of us never understand. Every obstacle presents an opportunity to improve our condition.

It is a fact of life that obstacles and resistances exist in many forms.

As I will say many times throughout these pages, you need to discipline your disappointment. When you get knocked back, you get back up, dust yourself down, appraise what has happened, if necessary tweak your plan and continue.

This of course does assume that what you are pursuing is a worthy goal. If you correctly followed the steps in the previous chapter and embarked on a journey towards your goal then you more than likely will want to continue.

You may of course change direction or re-appraise your final goal, but you will persevere nonetheless.

As a lesson in perseverance, let's see if you can guess who this person was?

He had to work to support his family after they were forced out of their home.	1816
His mother died.	1818
His business collapsed.	1831
Was defeated for legislature.	1832
Lost his job and failed to get into college.	1832
Declared bankruptcy, and spent the next 17 years of his life paying off the money he borrowed from friends to start his business.	1833
Was defeated for legislature again.	1834
Was engaged to be married, but his fiancée died.	1835
Had a nervous breakdown and spent the next six months in bed.	1836
Was defeated in becoming the speaker of the state legislature.	1838
Was defeated in becoming elector.	1840

Was defeated for Congress	1843
Was defeated for Congress.	1846
Was defeated for Congress again.	1848
Was rejected for the job of Land Officer in his home state.	1849
Was defeated for Senate.	1854
Was defeated for Vice-President -- got less than 100 votes.	1856
Was defeated for Senate for the third time.	1858
Was elected President of the United States.	1860

The man in question was Abraham Lincoln. Yes, a remarkable man and no, your goal may not be to become President, Prime Minister or even Head Chef.

What it does illustrate is that knock backs will happen.

It's how you respond that is important.

We will all lose a parent in life. That is a part of life. How you choose to pick yourself up and shape your life afterwards is the important thing.

The individual cannot directly influence the obstacles they meet but they can choose their reaction to them.

In the words of Jim Rohn:

"The wind blows the same way for all of us. It all depends on how you set your sail."

We need to learn how to objectively view the challenges which you encounter in your life.

Here, you will learn some coping skills and techniques which allow you to place your challenges in perspective, in relation to your goals.

You will learn to discipline your disappointment and gain a certain degree of wisdom and detachment to narrow expectations providing you with a more flexible and subtle view of the world which allows you to ebb and flow with the changes and challenges of life.

You will learn to ultimately view the majority of challenges as opportunities for growth and as stepping stones and lessons which you must overcome in order to achieve their goal.

But there is suffering in life, and there are defeats. No one can avoid them. But it's better to lose some of the battles in the struggles for your dreams than to be defeated without ever knowing what you're fighting for.

- Paulo Coelho

Obstacles are a fact of life

In a world of 6.7+ billion people all trying to get where they want to go, it is absolutely inevitable there are going to be obstacles, negotiations, disagreements and resistance in many forms.

Right here, right now, accept that it is a fact of life that you will encounter obstacles and challenges throughout your life journey.

If you're not meeting obstacles then you're not going anywhere. Treat obstacles as positive signs that you are on the move somewhere.

You will encounter obstacles. There are stepping stones and lessons you will frequently encounter which you cannot ignore or hide from if you are to progress onto your goal.

A hermit living in his cave is not going to really encounter a great variety of obstacles is he?

The only reason you have not already achieved your goal is because you have to pass these tests and experience these growths in order to get there.

It's like if you're goal is to compete at a national level at athletics and the powers that be have responded by saying, "Sure, absolutely, now all you have to do is train for the next 12 months, gradually achieve the required times and you're in."

Now, the correct and rational response to that would be "Great, I now have a clear path and sequence of steps to follow and although I won't get there on the first day, I will eventually if I stick to my task!"

However, because many of us either didn't have a clear conscious goal or have lost sight of it, we instead treat the response as a disaster. "What? I've to train for a year, and probably lose 80% of my races?! I give up!"

So, from here on in, I'd like you to keep in mind, that very often, the obstacles you encounter are simply necessary steps you need to fulfil before you can enjoy your goal.

So, that's what we're after here today. We're looking to unearth diamonds from the heaps of sooty coal you often face.

It's not about denial, it's not about blind optimism. It's about earnestly looking at the situation before you and asking yourself:

- What does this mean, in relation to my goal?

- How does this affect my goals, desires and wishes?

- How does this really affect my life?

- What are my options here?

- What else can this mean?

It's called reframing. It's about getting as many positive and optional perspectives on your "obstacle" and then deciding what choices lay before you.

We'll be looking at each of these elements in turn.

What we're looking for is to help you develop a disciplined and flexible mind that serves you and for you to become master of your mind.

In any situation, the person with the most flexibility and most options has the power.

We're looking to give you the power.

We're going to give you the power and the ability to decide whether a challenge or obstacle needs to be engaged and experienced or simply side-stepped.

Discipline, wisdom, flexibility and power.

Remember, you play the lead role in your life. If it helps, you can look at it like a video game. To get to the next level you need to pick up more prizes or pass more tests, otherwise, you stay on the same level.

Growth and improvement requires change and change always meets resistance.

Homeostasis

Before we continue, I'm going to bore you with some technical stuff.

Just as it is a fact of life that everything and everyone, including you, is in a constant state of change and growth, so also it is a fact of life that life itself, and the systems which support life, resist change to a certain degree.

There is a term called Homeostasis. Homeostasis simply means resistance to change.

Every system in the universe is subject to homeostasis.

Social, economic, ecogological, psychological, everything.

It's all the means by which nature tries to prevent chaos and likes to maintain smooth transition and smooth growth.

A case of evolution instead of revolution.

It's the same as those damper systems on doors that prevent them from banging or from slamming on someone's hands. It's there for our protection.

So, before we continue, become aware of that fact of its existence. Although it can manifest in seemingly challenging ways, it is in fact there for your benefit.

Homeostasis…

The biggest step to take, right here, right now, is to give yourself permission to change. Be willing to accept positive change in your life and be willing to seek out positive change.

There is a part in everyone's mind which is responsible for managing and controlling change in their lives.

In the past, that may have been primarily concerned with resisting change, but now, as you are forward directed and choosing life direction, that part is now undergoing a change into seeking out positive change and deciding which changes it wants for your life.

Improvement is a change.

Improvement is good.

Change is good.

QED…

Choose Your Battles Wisely

Before we learn how to view and overcome obstacles and challenges, it's helpful to first of all filter out exactly which of the obstacles are for our attention.

An example I have used before with relation to gaining perspective on obstacles is the following:

If you are driving between Dublin and Cork and you hear on the news that the bridge over the River Shannon in Athlone was closed, how would you feel?

You shouldn't really care. It shouldn't upset you in the least as it's not on your journey.

You're heading to Cork. Keep going.

You can choose to get upset about many things in the world, but if they are not in your circle of influence, let it go. Don't go there.

The same can be applied to many of your obstacles in life.

How do they relate to your goals? Where do they lie in relation to you getting to your chosen destination?

So, step one, you're going to learn to filter out the challenges, obstacles and opportunities that are yours to deal with.

You have a circle of influence and a circle of concern and you're going to learn to synchronise them.[6]

The result of which is that you are going to find that you might not have half enough things to worry about during day from now on. And wouldn't that be terrible ☺

---

6   For more on Circle of Concern/Influence, check out Stephen R. Covey

Before we move on from this point, keep in mind, our discussion on those Six Needs we all have.

If you feel compelled to always take up a challenge, regardless of whether it is really for you or not, then maybe, just maybe, there's a need being met in a slightly neurotic manner on your part...?

Just something to consider for you.

Leave it to the birds

We often feel an ego-driven need to exert control on certain things or to engage in certain struggles to prove ourselves.

To prove ourselves. That's a crucial point.

You don't need to prove yourself in anyway, to anyone!

You simply need to be happy, that's it.

At this point, after your work on your needs, values and motivations, we will have hopefully filtered out much of the ego-driven garbage anyway but there is loads left for us to work on now.

Our ego often makes us take on challenges so as to prove to ourselves "that we can" or to prove to others "that we're good enough".

Tip for today. Let it go. Don't go there. Ego-driven engagement of challenges is a distraction.

To use an analogy.

A farmer is out planting seeds in his field. As he plants them. The birds come down and start to feed themselves.

What should the farmer do? Spend his time chasing the birds or simply continue with his sowing?

Which course of action will eventually get him his harvest?

Let the birds have their share. Don't go chasing them.[7]

The importance of having your goal

This again, is why it is so important to have your goals and purpose.

If you have no point of focus for your attention, no focus of desire and energy, then it can be very easy to feel "at-sea" and lost when you encounter challenges and obstacles.

As the saying goes, "if you don't know which direction you're heading in, no wind is favourable".

It's easy to imagine it really. If you have no sense of self, direction and have no idea where you are going or why you are going there, how on earth can you have the presence of mind to look at challenges and opportunities objectively? Everything loses context and perspective.

On the other hand, when you are centred, have your direction, focused goals and desire, you can withstand the buffeting and the knocks as you have your eye on the prize all along the way.

---

7   Thanks to the late Jim Rohn for this little metaphor

How does my challenge relate to my goal?

So, you've encountered a situation that threatens to put you in bad form or threatens to knock you off track. That's an important thought, Off-Track.

Whenever you encounter your obstacle, are you on a track? And if so, where is that track leading to?

You cannot control everything that happens to you, but you always, always have both the ability and the responsibility to choose your reaction to it and your thoughts about it.

You are looking to develop a curiosity about the things that happen to you.

You are looking to remove all pre-programmed impulsive reactions or judgements.

You are looking to disable negative automatic responses to problems. Many of your responses to challenges have become automatic conditioned responses, developed over time.

You are now going to reclaim the power and responsibility for your responses.

From now on, you're going to learn to be detached, in a way, from the challenges that occur. This objective detachment is going to buy you time, as it were, to do a little comparison between what has happened, what it means and what bearing it really has on where you are heading.

To repeat the point here, you are trying to learn whether the challenge that you face is really your concern or not?

So, the general outline you will learn to follow is:

1. **What area of my life does this problem/challenge effect?**

2. **Which of my goals or intentions does this challenge effect?**

3. **What are my options in relation to this challenge?**

A major question you can ask yourself in relation to this issue is:

"If I did nothing, what would be the outcome?"

Direct Obstacles on your Path

And then, there are the fears and obstacles that stand right in your face. You can try to side-step them, but they also side-step to face you again.

You try to walk around them, but they don't let you pass.

Your biggest obstacles, challenges and fears. They are the gatekeeper to your future. To cross the bridge, as it were, you must answer the questions asked of you.

If that seems simplistic and if you're thinking, "that's all well and good in theory but the practice is more difficult", then, yes, I agree but it is still the reality.

Take a young man, who feared public speaking, who stammered and was generally petrified of even asking questions in a classroom.

This same young man also had a goal, an ambition, to teach, lecture, to give speeches.

So you have his goal in direct opposition to his fear. There is no side stepping, there is no avoiding it, unless you give up.

The fear has to be engaged and overcome if you wish to proceed onto your goal.

Now in one case, the stammering, shyness and nervousness can be seen as being a huge obstacle in front of the goal.

But if you flip that over and reframe it, if the fear of speaking, if the stammering is fixed, then voila, you have all the skills and resources ready to pursue your goal.

As the saying goes, "*if there is something you feel you **can't** do, then that is something you **must** do!*"

Oh, by the way, that man is me.

Very often, our biggest fears are the most important lessons which we need to learn.

The bigger the obstacle the bigger the reward.

The bigger the obstacle, the bigger your dreams.

Personally, I find that if you're encountering huge obstacles, it's a positive sign that you're on your way to huge advances in your life, because after you have overcome your seemingly huge obstacle, you yourself have taken a quantum leap forward and your world leaps with it.

So, your learning point here is:

If there is a fear or an obstacle which seems to persist in your life and "keeps getting in your way", don't try to run from it, don't try to avoid it, it's a lesson which you need to learn and overcome.

Getting a Perspective on your obstacles

A problem or obstacle is only as big as your mind makes it.

Already some of you are thinking of a major issue in your life, maybe even an illness or bereavement and you are thinking "he's talking rubbish, this is huge!!"

What has happened has happened. Your mind can make it better or worse and your decision as to how you want to view and address your problem will determine how the issue progresses.

It comes down to the issue where the same calamity can happen to two different people and they can react very differently to it.

There is always a choice in how you react.

It is necessary to gain a mental perspective on the issue, discipline your disappointment.

It's important to accept that when something happens, no matter how bad it is, it has happened.

It is necessary to separate yourself from the problem. You are not the problem. The problem is not you. It is an external entity, so look to separate yourself from it.

Stand back so as you can evaluate the problem, size it up for options.

Don't allow yourself to be engulfed by the problem or challenge.

Again, it is not you. Treat is as a separate object.

It's important to realise that somewhere, somebody else experienced the same problem and overcame it. You have a choice; do you wish to overcome the problem?

Of course you do. If you didn't, then you wouldn't care about the problem, and then it wouldn't be a problem.

You also have the responsibility to find the solution. You can of course get help on it, but ultimately, it's your choice and your responsibility and this presents you with the power and the permission to choose.

By gaining a perspective on a problem, you discipline your mind and you then have access to possible solutions and are flexible enough to look at different ways to solve the problem.

Worrying is completely useless.

If it is within your power to fix something, then why worry, go ahead and fix it.

If it is not within your power to fix something, then what's the point in worrying?

From now on, at all times, you are looking for solutions. From now on, every time you encounter a "problem", you are immediately looking at possible solutions and are thinking of the benefits of finding the solution, and sometimes the solution is to do nothing at all…

Questions to Ponder

Think of a challenge that persists in your life or a situation that seems to continuously cause you pain.

How would your life be different if this situation did not exist?

If you overcame this problem, how would your life improve?

How would overcoming this problem influence your major life goals?

What is the one thing you are NOT prepared to do to resolve this issue?

Name one positive and productive change you can make now with relation to the issue?

If you did not nothing what would be the possible outcomes?

Two monks were once travelling together down a muddy road. A heavy rain was falling. Coming around a bend, they met a lovely girl in a silk kimono and sash, unable to cross the intersection.

"Come on, girl," said the first monk. Lifting her in his arms, he carried her over the mud.

The second monk did not speak again until that night when they reached a lodging temple. Then he no longer could restrain himself. "We monks don't go near females," he said. "It is dangerous. Why did you do that?"

"I left the girl there," the first monk said. "Are you still carrying her?"

Before we continue

Congratulations to you for getting this far. You've stuck with it and even if you've gotten a little tired in places, you're still already undergoing a change. Even if you decided to forget everything you've read you can't. It's in there now, and like an itch, all of those questions you've read and asked of yourself will be off an infinite Google search to find answers.

Your journey so far has explored why your life and indeed, your country needs you to become the best that you can be.

We've explored the opportunity that awaits you should you decide to accept the challenge of being the best that you can be.

We've looked at your deeper self, your values, priorities and philosophies in life.

We've looked at some of your strengths in life.

We've looked at how to set effective goals in your life and even how to overcome obstacles that may appear in your path.

So, what comes next?

Next, we're going to take this new you and place you back out there, in the world and see how the new you, the real you, the old you, fits back into the world and begins to effect the world and effect your life in the world.

We'll look at the opportunities that await you and some of the strategies and philosophies which you can adopt to take all of these nice theories and ideas and make them actually matter in the real world.

And by all means, if you haven't had too much already, you can go for another coffee now.

Back to the Real World

The Principle of Service

I never see what has been done; I only see what remains to be done.

- Marie Curie

Learning from the past is not always the way to create the future. Sometimes a complete paradigm shift is needed.

Henry Ford once commented that most people's solutions to transport issues at the start of the 20th century centred on "more horses".

He (along with the invention of Mr Diesel) actually brought in a brand new era, unconstrained by what had come before.

I ask you to do the same.

I ask you to not check and gauge your ideas on measurements or references which came before, but to imagine absolutely fresh ideas, fresh ways of doing things, fresh ways of dealing with people.

History should perhaps best be used to teach us what "not to do", as opposed what to do.

Imagination, genius and an individual and collective sense of purpose create the future.

It is my belief (so you can dismiss it if you wish) that many of our ills have been caused by self-serving, looking after number one, and seeking profit merely for the sake of it.

Professor Charles Handy asked the question, "when is enough, enough?" If we never know when enough is enough, then how can you truly value anything and how can you really create any sort of society which is meant to serve the people in it?

I want you to consider the concept of service as being of ultimate importance and ultimate virtue.

By service I do not mean being slave or being in servitude. By service I mean aspiring to a lofty ideal of serving something bigger than ourselves.

To some, it could simply be your football team. That is service.

To some it could be their community group.

Service is about contributing to the whole.

What you contribute and what that whole is, is entirely up to you.

Like I told you at the beginning, you make the rules.

What if our companies, banks and indeed governments truly operated out of a sense of service?

Indeed aren't they meant to?

I made reference earlier that the Grail Code, much hyped in the Da Vinci Code, was actually nothing to do with a chalice but instead represented a code of honour, the Grail Code, the Code of Service.

It was said that this code lived on through the Merovingian Royal Dynasty, down through the Stuarts and allegedly into some of the royal families of Europe.

That was the intention, but like much else, power corrupts I guess.

We talked earlier about values and priorities and philosophies and we asked, what is sacred to you?

What is sacred to you? What do you feel a sense of service to?

It can be anything.

What I am suggesting to you now is that whatever you do endeavour to do, whatever you plan to create individually and collectively, do so with the principle of service.

Create your companies and life structures around being of service and giving more than you receive and ironically you will receive far more.

The evidence has blatantly shown that to take more than you give results in us all being driven to ruin.

Look around you, it hasn't worked.

You've came on quite a journey in this book and there's not much left to go, but before we finish, think again about you, as an individual, and now, think for a moment about how you plug back into the collective.

Think about how you will contribute back to the collective, taking some courageous risks in connecting with people, in sharing yourself and in dealing with perceived setbacks in a positive way.

Think about how you can create, with others, something of true value.

We are here on earth to do good for others. What the others are here for, I don't know.

- W. H. Auden

The next section gets you focused on you and your individual sense of purpose, value and what you can bring to the world.

We will then look at the collective effect.

You are the product

Without getting bogged down in any talk of money, ultimately your success in life can come down to you seeing yourself as something or someone of value, a product or a service provider.

This does not mean that to be successful you need to make money.

What I mean is that you already have some way of touching people's lives and contributing to people's lives and that in a sense makes you a unique product, with a value that people need.

Apart from the personal value of that, which we have looked at, there is of course the very real opportunity for you to turn "you" into your own business by developing you as the product.

You have skills, talents and unique characteristics that you take for granted every single day.

Whether you realise it or not, you already have a gift or a talent that somebody else is already paying for.

You already have hobbies, interests and passions in life that are so second nature to you, that you may be ignoring them.

If you have a hobby that you are passionate about, search on Google to see how many businesses there are doing exactly that.

The future of business in this country and worldwide is no longer going to be about lifetime jobs in large corporations, working until you are 65, but instead will be about independent businesses providing niche services and products, which all draw together to fulfil greater market needs.

It will be about the strategic collaboration of independent experts. We all need to become independent experts and valuable products and providing a service of some kind.

And that's the crucial point. Service.

When you are being of service, using your unique gifts and talents with passion, you are guaranteed a life of success and abundance.

When you are working at something about which you are truly passionate and in which you truly believe, you will attract all of the people, resources and help you require.

You will find yourself easily, naturally, and automatically drifting into groups of like-minded people, and you will experience synergy, where the collective gifts and talents of a group of people with a common dream and passion create something far greater than any of the individuals would have ever dreamed of.

Instead of work becoming your life, your life will be your greatest work.

Your life will be an ongoing, continuously improving work in progress.

The first step is to have that passion. Then believe in it, and develop it. Believe in your own absolutely unique way of thinking. The more unique it is, the more brilliant it is.

If you can dream it, you can do it.

The more unlike common convention it is, the more groundbreaking and revolutionary it is and that is what you are after.

When you work at something you love, with those goose bumps, you will never work a day in your life and you will attract abundance, profits and good fortune.

Real abundance and success in life and in business comes from contributing or providing a service. All top entrepreneurs had the dream, not of making pots of cash, but of providing a new service to people.

What is your service? What can you already contribute, now?

What can you do right this minute that is of use and is second nature to you?

We've talked about your value, your purpose, your mind, what makes you unique and we've even wrote a Mission Statement.

At this point, you know a whole lot more about who are and what you are about than you did before you picked up this book.

So, now the 6.75 billion dollar question, what is your unique selling point? This is tighter and compact and shorter than your Mission statement.

This is your killer elevator pitch that leaves the person who hears it in absolutely no doubt what you can do.

It can be very simple.

For some, it could be the best mechanic around.

You could be the best singer that you know.

You could be anything.

Personally, I'd shy away from the concept of being the "best" anything apart from being the best that you can be. Once you start thinking in competitive terms, you've already placed some of your energy and focus on your imaginary competitors leaving less for you.

Focus on you here.

What is your unique selling point?

What is your true value?

What problems can you solve for people?

What makes you stand out from the crowd?

What can you do easily and naturally so that it doesn't even seem like an effort?

What would you happily spend your life doing, not even thinking about retirement or pensions?

Isn't it heartbreaking when we think of the world we live in where so many people are working in jobs they hate, just to live, and looking forward to the age of 65 when they retire?

It's like a jail sentence.

If you had all the money in the world, and when you got tired of the yachts and the champagne, what would you spend your time doing?

If there was no such thing as money and the only way you could buy goods and services was to use your unique selling point and service what would that be?

When you think about your younger days, hanging out with your friends, what was the "role" you easily filled, what were you good at?

Think back to the goose bump moments we discussed, what were they?

Think back to your values and what was sacred to you in life. What were those things?

What were the things you would not sacrifice for anything?

These are all clues to the real, inner you, what makes you unique and what you can develop into your service.

Your unique selling point can have two portions.

One is your unique personal qualities that provide you with the ability to effectively work with people and form relationships and communicate effectively to get things done and to create opportunities for yourself.

The second is your skill set, your natural talent combined with the persistence and discipline we talked about.

Isn't it far easier to work hard and apply yourself to something that you love doing, and when you're doing it for you?

It doesn't have to be hard work either but a labour of love.

Saints and Scholars, hearts and minds.

The answers to these questions might not appear now, or in the next half hour but from this moment on you're going to find yourself becoming more aware of the patterns in life that tell you more about your strengths and you're going to find yourself becoming more aware of your unique selling points and how you can develop them further.

This is all about focusing your sense of self even more in relation to your unique value and to highlight within your own mind what you have to offer the world.

Once you are clear of this, then in a following section, you will see how this then helps you to collaborate with other like minded individuals and create a combined success.

Step one though is for you to become absolutely clear and certain about what you do and what you offer. It is then that opportunities come your way and it is then that you spot open doors for your talents.

Collaboration and Success Building

The 100th Monkey

Let me tell you a little story…

The Japanese monkey, Macaca Fuscata, had been observed in the wild for a period of over 30 years.

In 1952, on the island of Koshima, scientists were providing monkeys with sweet potatoes dropped in the sand. The monkey liked the taste of the raw sweet potatoes, but they found the dirt unpleasant.

An 18-month-old female named Imo found she could solve the problem by washing the potatoes in a nearby stream. She taught this trick to her mother. Her playmates also learned this new way and they taught their mothers too.

This cultural innovation was gradually picked up by various monkeys before the eyes of the scientists. Between 1952 and 1958 all the young monkeys learned to wash the sandy sweet potatoes to make them more palatable. Only the adults who imitated their children learned this social improvement. Other adults kept eating the dirty sweet potatoes.

Then something startling took place. In the autumn of 1958, a certain number of Koshima monkeys were washing sweet potatoes -- the exact number is not known. Let us suppose that when the sun rose one morning there were 99 monkeys on Koshima Island who had learned to wash their sweet potatoes.

Let's further suppose that later that morning, the hundredth monkey learned to wash potatoes.

THEN IT HAPPENED!

By that evening almost everyone in the tribe was washing sweet potatoes before eating them. The added energy of this hundredth monkey somehow created an ideological breakthrough!

But notice: A most surprising thing observed by these scientists was that the habit of washing sweet potatoes then jumped over the sea...Colonies of monkeys on other islands and the mainland troop of monkeys at Takasakiyama began washing their sweet potatoes.

Thus, when a certain critical number achieves an awareness, a quorum, this new awareness may be communicated from mind to mind.

Although the exact number may vary, this Hundredth Monkey Phenomenon means that when only a limited number of people know of a new way, it may remain the conscious property of these people.

But there is a point at which if only one more person tunes-in to a new awareness, a field is strengthened so that this awareness is picked up by almost everyone!

So why did I tell you that story?

It's all about knowing when and how to brainstorm and when and how to collaborate.

It is essential that you are both completely aware of your own unique strengths and talents and that you know how and when to collaborate with others in order to achieve your ultimate goals and success.

There are many goals you can achieve yourself, such as developing your own personal qualities such as confidence etc. However, when it comes to achieving success in projects, teams and even businesses, it is fairly much impossible to achieve great success without collaborating with others and accepting and understanding that we live in an inter-dependent world.

We all have something to contribute and when we all get together in the right way at the right time, the sum total of the collaboration of the individual parts can far outweigh the individual parts.

You have already covered the concept of your unique selling point, so you are now more aware of what you have to contribute to your life and to the community and world at large.

Now, we look at the power of collaboration and harnessing your own creative thoughts in an independent manner.

The 100th Monkey story powerfully illustrates that when the time is right for an idea or a concept, and when a critical mass is achieved, things can take on a life of their own in ways that even science is finding difficult to fully explain.

When you are ready to launch yourself the people you need to support you will strangely be there already, but when you are ready.

Very often, when we are not ready, and we attempt to collaborate with others to begin with, we can often take a back seat, hide our own ideas and not fully access our creative resources.

What begins with your very own creative idea ends up as you simply agreeing with somebody else's.

This is not wrong in its own right, but it is so much more fulfilling and effective for you if you have first done the inner work and carried out your own exhaustive brainstorming of your concept and idea.

You will then know (by following the goal setting template) what you may need from a collaboration with others.

You know what you have to offer.

You will then know your boundary and you will know when to say no when necessary.

When you work from this direction, you will actually find yourself "accidentally" discovering or crossing paths with exactly the like minded people who complement your strengths and contributions.

You will discover the other monkeys if you like ☺

It will seem like magic or telepathy, but the 100th monkey story tells you why.

Dare to dream and know beyond any doubt that if your dream is based on who you truly are, your passions and your gifts, it will become reality and you will begin to witness "Synchronistic Events" in your everyday life.

Synchronicity is yet another phenomenon in our world that science has not yet explained, debunked or agreed with, yet it happens all the time.

You know those times when you are idly thinking of somebody and all of a sudden, the phone rings and it's them?

Or when you have been humming a song to yourself and you turn the radio on and it's playing?

We've all experienced it and we're not sure how it happens.

There are many theories, including some by the great Carl Gustav Jung who propose that there is another level of consciousness beyond our individual unconscious mind, which he called "The collective unconscious" and it was his belief that from time to time, we connect with this universal stream of consciousness and attract the things we think about.

But there is a condition to the workings of the unconscious and beyond.

When you simply "try really hard" to make something happen from your ego, with your main thought being about "why isn't it working?" it doesn't seem to work.

It seems from universal experience that it happens almost accidentally with casual thoughts where you had no fixed attachment to anything happening.

And that's a crucial element.

When you have set a goal, for the right reasons, according to your gifts, values, dreams and desires, and when that goal is for your highest good and for the highest good of other people effected by it, and when you have done your best, and taken action on the work steps you set out, you then let go, and release your attachment to the outcome.

There are many books written on this topic so I won't go off on a tangent now, but be aware of it, and in terms of collaboration and meeting the people you need to meet in life, know that there's no need to force the outside world to do anything.

Do the inner and personal work first and what's yours will not pass you by.

Take your goals and your dreams, live your life by them and accept whatever comes your way as feedback.

Seek to take your goals and dreams to the world and to work with others.

As I mentioned before, look upon yourself as a contractor or consultant with a particular service to contribute and the more problems you can solve in the world, the more valuable you become.

The more people's lives you touch, the more important you become.

To touch people's lives you must get in touch with yourself, raise your personal awareness and accept yourself.

It all comes back to you in the end and the work you do on yourself and for yourself will be your greatest masterpiece.

You can be both that Saint and that Scholar. Touching people's lives and creating a new world.

Master mind Groups and Networking

Your generation has another small advantage over those who came before.

You are the first generation to grow up networked, connected, online.

Through the likes of Bebo, Facebook, MySpace and more, you can connect to literally thousands of like minded people throughout the world, in every culture.

Can you imagine how difficult it must have been for somebody back in the 1960s to connect to 2,000 people before they were 19?

Impossible.

But think of how much more powerful these networks can be if you use them for more than your holiday photographs?

The possibilities are endless. Advertising companies are abandoning traditional TV and Print media because you guys aren't interested.

You are interested in what your friends are interested in.

You are already creating communities, interest groups and mini-nations online and this is where the world's corporations are trying to get in.

They know that if they can connect with a portion of your network, your group, the rest of you might follow.

But here's something better.

This again connects into the concept that we are all connected either economically, ecologically, digitally or some other way.

Your increase in awareness to this point has also increased your sense of responsibility due to the fact that we are all connected and now that becoming connected has become so natural to you, the boundaries you maintain are more fluid and seamless, but you can also learn to navigate that and dance with that as you create your own sense of responsibility based around who you know yourself to be and what you have to share with others.

You have the ability to exchange ideas, start campaigns, advertise yourself and much more by simply sending a message to your contact list.

It's phenomenal if it's used right.

Can you imagine how the world will be in even 5 years time if you take control of this networking possibility?

A generation of entrepreneurs, connected, collaborating and networking.

Independent geniuses, who are self aware, gifted in one or more of the areas of intelligence, who are aware of their strengths and passions in life, all coming together to exchange ideas, meet like minded people, creating groups, creating companies, creating political movements, creating whatever the hell you want.

There are 450,000 people on the unemployment register in Ireland currently. Are you telling me that by plugging all of your brains and energy together, we can't create something great for this country and beyond?

My tip for you now is to begin to chat to your friends and create Master Mind groups. Discussion groups with people of like mind and complementary talents who discuss the possibilities of the day, and come up with ideas for the future and then work towards creating goals and achieving them.

You have all the tools you need here in this book to do that.

Your teachers will be more than willing to help because a healthy and motivated classroom makes their job easier and they'll be happy to at last be doing what they started teaching to do.

Talk to your friends and arrange to meet in someone's house, once a week.

Research a famous inventor or historical figure. Find out what made them tick.

Ask questions. Email me if you like. I'd be delighted to help you out.

Nobody is going to do this for you and nobody is going to create your life for you.

This is in your own hands and that's a positive thing.

Don't let time pass by, make a call now, send an email, create a Facebook, Bebo or MySpace group.

Become a leader of your own idea today and invite others to share the journey. Who knows where it will end, and who knows what national or global issue you will solve?

And if you stay focused on the passion, the mission, being of service and serving a higher value, you will end up in a place far better than you could have imagined.

Business Ideas for your to work with

The main purpose of this book was not to simply create businesses but to create better people who create better businesses, better families, better everything.

A good business that provides a good service, and solves problems and makes people's lives better is an obvious good thing.

If it makes you fabulously wealthy and famous as well, then fantastic.

The chapter heading was a bit of a trick.

You don't need me to give you ideas on businesses or ventures in order to create something wonderful.

That's why you have your imagination, creativity and natural abilities.

You already have ideas in your head that you dismissed many times.

Take them back out, dust them off and share them with others and start getting to work on them.

When you develop these ideas, then perhaps you can actually choose a college course related to your natural skills and interests.

How cool would it be to be able to say "I chose XXX on my CAO so that I could grow and expand my business"?

I don't know many people who can say that, with the exception of mature students who go back to college on a full salary from their employer.

Choose your mission and your vision, start your plan, set some goals, and then choose either your college course or some sort of mentoring program with a related business.

Become experts and masters in your chosen field and be sure that you will never be out of work and every hour you work you will enjoy.

There is no age limit to being happy, fulfilled and successful.

A new image for Ireland

I didn't want to finish things off with putting any pressure on you, but your country needs you for a whole other reason.

Our image abroad has been tarnished and we look a little foolish right now.

You have an opportunity to redress that, and it doesn't even require you to be a multi-millionaire.

It requires that you be a good person, clear of purpose, self-confident yes, but also humble, grateful, graceful and self-aware.

It requires that you know your place in the world and know your value in the world.

It requires that you accept that you are an ambassador for yourself, your family and your country and that this is a responsibility you take great pride in.

We are a truly unique country and people in one sense, in terms of our views on the world, our philosophies, our people, our sense of humour and more.

We have gone through many changes in the last decade or more and that is a good thing, because just as you need to flourish and thrive as an individual first and then step out into the world and contribute to the whole, Ireland as a country needs to undertake a similar journey.

A country is its people.

As a country and a people, we need to re-discover what makes us unique, and what defines us, in an inclusive way.

We need to re-discover what connects us to other people, other cultures and other nations.

We need to re-discover what we can contribute to the whole and this can only happen if we undergo that discovery on a personal level first, as you have now begun to do.

So what does it mean to be Irish in the 21st century?

What values, philosophies, beliefs and behaviours form what you believe we can be?

What do we hold dear and what should we hold dear?

We are no longer an isolated rock off the west coast of Europe but we are also no longer the nouveau riche of the world. That was a delusional journey, one from which we have learned many lessons.

So, we're back to a new plateau, one from which we can rise again, and create something new.

To create something new, you must create something new, our people must create something new.

Our core essence may not have changed however, in the same way that your core values and philosophies may not have changed.

It's more a matter of becoming aware of what they are and being able to articulate and communicate that message in a way that is expansive, constructive and inclusive.

As I stated back at the beginning, we have fought no major conflicts with other nations, we do not have a recognised list of "enemies", and we do not have significant natural resources such as precious metals or fossil fuels.

What we do have is people and people are creative, people are capable and people are different in many ways but similar in more.

There is no reason why our people cannot be of the highest possible calibre, with well developed intelligence in whatever area of life, and also well developed as personalities.

We cannot wait for governments to create you in their image.

It is you who must create the image of who you wish to be and to then take the steps, with the support of your peers, towards that image or vision you may have.

You have an opportunity to bring in a new era of Saints and Scholars for our country and I wish you every success in doing that in whatever pursuit you choose.

When you look back

This is the true joy in life, the being used for a purpose recognized by yourself as a mighty one; the being thoroughly worn out before you are thrown on the scrap heap; the being a force of nature instead of a feverish selfish little clod of ailments and grievances complaining that the world will not devote itself to making you happy.

- G.B. Shaw

What do you truly wish for your life to be? Have you ever really thought about it?

When you are old and grey, and looking back over your life, what do you want it to have looked like?

One of my ambitions in life is to be thoroughly exhausted but satisfied when the time comes to pass on.

What I do not want is to have loads left to do but not to have the energy to do it.

Worse again, I do not want to have regrets over not doing something for some trivial reason that seemed important at the time.

But enough of what I don't want.

What I do want is to know that I lived each day as me. I want to rest in the knowledge that I didn't hide, I didn't pretend and I didn't hide my light under that very crowded bushel.

I want to know that if I had a thought or an idea that would help even one other person that I would use it, cultivate it and even if I couldn't produce a physical result from it, I would pass it to someone who could.

What do you want your life to be?

I want to look back and accept that there were many wonderful people in my life, but that ultimately I made the decisions that belonged to me and did not abdicate my responsibility to others.

I want to know that I questioned myself, asked more of myself and took responsibility for myself.

I want to know that I accepted the challenge to be me.

I accept that not everything turned out as planned, but that I still got up, dusted myself down and as long as I had a breath in my body and a thought in my mind, there was life to be lived.

I'm not asking you to save the world or save your country.

I'm not asking you to take on the burden of securing the future for us all but I am asking you to be honest with yourself and be you and make sure that the world knew you existed and that you gave the best of you, if not for others, then at least for you.

Be a Saint and a Scholar, and use your heart and your head together to become more.

And remember…

Be More… Do More…. And you shall Have more…

In life, many thoughts are born in the course of a moment, an hour, a day. Some are dreams, some visions. Often, we are unable to distinguish between them. To some, they are the same; however, not all dreams are visions. Much energy is lost in fanciful dreams that never bear fruit. But visions are messages from the Great Spirit, each for a different purpose in life. Consequently, one person's vision may not be that of another. To have a vision, one must be prepared to receive it, and when it comes, to accept it. Thus when these inner urges become reality, only then can visions be fulfilled. The spiritual side of life knows everyone's heart and who to trust. How could a vision ever be given to someone to harbor if that person could not be trusted to carry it out. The message is simple: commitment precedes vision.

The mere possession of a vision is not the same as living it, nor can we encourage others with it if we do not, ourselves, understand and follow its truths. The pattern of the Great Spirit is over us all, but if we follow our own spirits from within, our pattern becomes clearer. For centuries, others have sought their visions. They prepare themselves, so that if the Creator desires them to know their life's purpose, then a vision would be revealed. To be blessed with visions is not enough…we must live them!

- High Eagle:

About the Author

Gavin G Gregan is a Business and Personal Coach, Clinical Psychotherapist and Hypnotherapist with many years of experience in helping people achieve their dreams. The pursuit of a life of purpose and authenticity lies at the heart of Gavin's work. Born and resident in Ireland, his interest and curiousity in the human condition has resulted in a lifetime of dedication in the pursuit of happiness for everyone he encounters on this life journey.

Lightning Source UK Ltd.
Milton Keynes UK
16 March 2010

151454UK00001B/6/P